THE GODSTONE & THE BLACKYMOR

THE GODSTONE
AND THE BLACKYMOR

by T. H. WHITE

illustrated by EDWARD ARDIZZONE

JONATHAN CAPE
Thirty Bedford Square · London

Class no- 828·91408

9999030767✓

FIRST PUBLISHED 1959
© 1959 BY T. H. WHITE
ILLUSTRATIONS © 1959 BY JONATHAN CAPE LTD

PRINTED IN GREAT BRITAIN BY
BUTLER & TANNER LTD, FROME, SOMERSET
BOUND BY A. W. BAIN & CO. LTD, LONDON

Contents

Love to Dawn

RAOCH was a shooting lodge which had belonged to a whisky baron. For fifty pounds a month whoever rented it was monarch of about ten thousand acres which claimed to be a grouse moor, and of several pools in a preserved salmon river. The salmon were there. You could see them leaping, leaping, from the low, warm, crystal water — like interplanetary rockets — and toppling back into it with a heart-thumping, sidelong swash. But they were impossible to catch, because of the golden weather. We basked by the river in a cloud of midges, tormented by the insects and by the unattainable fish. As for the famous grouse, at a generous estimate there may have been a hundred in all those thousands of acres. Several guns, ranging the mountains industriously all day behind a passable setter, might end with three or four brace. This made Fraoch a first-rate place for hawking.

If you are on one of the lordly Yorkshire grouse moors, where you can hardly walk ten paces without tripping over a pack of birds, it is redundant to use a setter. You find more grouse than you would ever carry, simply by walking forward. So you sit in a butt with a bottle of champagne, while the birds are driven over in bullet-paced streams. If you are on the starved tops of Mayo, however, you need a wide-ranging dog to find a shot at all. The same sort of thing applies to falconry. Different terrains suit different kinds of activity. It is no use flying merlins in strong heather or peregrines in woodland, because in each case the quarry can hide itself from the pursuer too easily to give a chance of catching it. Merlins need downland like Salisbury Plain, and peregrines need the moor. On the other hand, a peregrine on a well-stocked moor would not be interesting. She would have killed her maximum in half an hour or less, too easily, and it would be time to go home.

At Fraoch, where the rare, crafty and ancient grouse used to hobble about on crutches or sit before their heather cottages smoking broken clay pipes, with steel-rimmed spectacles over their rheumy eyes, spitting in the turf ashes and exchanging folklore about Niall of the Nine Hostages, it needed strong thighs to march the mountains and a high heart to circumvent them.

The Lodge stood at the end of a two mile drive or side road, in a bower of rhododendrons and fuchsias, looking out between their thick leaves across a dozen miles of bog to Crossmolina. No tree or house was visible from the overgrown lawn.

It was a charming, gimcrack house — shabbily, sparsely, comfortably furnished. It even had a working bathroom which worked with a roar, on some kind of geyser understood by the cook and the housemaids. Perhaps it was worked by Calor gas. The old-fashioned, broken-springed, second-hand, chintz-covered, welcoming armchairs had been brought somehow or other all the way from Dublin. As usual in Ireland, the ugly furniture was leavened here and there by a fine eighteenth-century piece, or by a cut-glass decanter. On the wall of the sitting room there was an amateur tracing of the outline of a fifteen-pound salmon. On a side table lay the game book with its few entries. The wash-hand-stands of the bedrooms were of the nineteenth century, and the old beds were deep and comfortable.

Surrounded by a sort of circular ambulatory or tunnel through the shiny leaves, which took twenty minutes or so to get round the lodge, Fraoch had two unsurpassable beauties.

On the mountain behind it, outside the shaded grounds in the sunshine, there was a minute waterfall or glide of water.

The soft, tart, ale-coloured stream slid over the smooth stones from step to step, cool and glistering in the late August heat. And the bogland plain which stretched to Crossmolina was held in a horseshoe of barren mountains which rose to about 2,500 feet. Behind us, Slieve Fyagh, Benmore and Maumakeogh nourished the grouse. Opposite the dining-room windows, Corslieve and the Nephin Beg range carried a loving eye to the distant sugar loaf of Nephin, 2,646 feet, whose summit I had once reached in solitude, carrying a peregrine tiercel panting in the sunlight.

Several of these heights had cairns on them. On Corslieve there was a laborious pile of stones called Leaghtdauhybaun — Fair David's Cairn — which was either in memory of a King Dathi who had been killed there by lightning in the year 427 or else of a blond robber called David, also slain there but by the military some thirteen hundred years later. Probably it was a prehistoric erection, taken over by the king and by the robber in their turns. It stood aloof, incredibly old and distant, against the lonely skyline.

It was an ancient landscape, which had few contacts with modern history. Away to the north-east, near Sligo, was the Rath where Eoghan Bel had been buried, killed in battle by the Ulstermen, fourteen hundred years before. He had been buried upright, standing with his spear in hand. After that, the Ulstermen had always been defeated when they reached his tumulus — until they had the presence of mind to dig him up again, and bury him upside down.

12

I liked to think that Slieve Fyagh, on which the lodge stood, was the place where Aillilbannda King of Connaught had fallen in the sixth century, at the battle of Cuilconaire. It was just possible to think so, for half the place names of Carra were interchangeable with those of Erris.

'As touching Ailillbannda, King of Connaught,' said the Book of Leinster about this monarch, 'the matter whereby he had the Lord's peace was this: the battle of Cuilconaire it was, which he fought against Clann Fiachrach and in which he was defeated, when he said to his charioteer: "Cast now, I pray thee, a look to the rear, and discover whether the killing be great and the slayers near us." The driver looked behind him and replied: "The slaughter that is made of the people is intolerable!" "Not their own guilt, but my pride and unrighteousness it is that comes against them," said the king: "wherefore turn we now the chariot to face the pursuers; for if I be slain, it will be the redemption of many." Then Ailill did earnest act of penance, and by his foemen fell. "That man therefore," said Columcille, "attained to the Lord's peace." '

At twice the distance of Nephin from us to the eastward, there was a different Corslieve in the Curlew Mountains. It also had a cairn, near which Young Donn had been killed in the year 1230, fighting against the foreigners. 'Donn Og, being then alone, was proclaimed and recognized; and many soldiers took aim, and five arrows were lodged in him; and one horseman came up with him afterwards; and though he had no weapon but an axe, he did not allow the horseman to close with him;

and the horseman would drive his lance into him occasionally. The other soldiers surrounded him from the east and west, and he fell by the superior power that overtook him there.'

For a view like this, which shared the Lord's peace with the derring-do of Ailill King of Connaught, fifty pounds a month did not seem too much. The Lodges which I sometimes rented were incidental to life in the West, not essential to it. But they were nice incidents.

'How many of these creatures have you trained?' Bunny asked, munching a sandwich in the high, bright air, as we rested for lunch.

'It depends what you mean by trained.'

I counted them on my fingers.

'If you include owls, and the ones I failed with, I have had thirteen. The most distinguished was a gyr-falcon. But I was only her owner on paper. I only saw her once. A sister of hers was flown to Germany as a present for General Goering, in one of those corrugated aeroplanes. He received her with pomp and circumstance.'

'Was she one of the ones which Ernest Vesey collected in Iceland?'

'I might have guessed you would know all about it.'

Bunny was the kindest, most educated, most formidable person I knew. Whenever I began to explain something to him, it was discouraging to find that he knew it already, and generally knew more than I did. Perhaps his dynasty was the last we shall see in literature, of altruistic, scholarly gentlemen of genius, who for generations had sought out the struggling authors like D. H. Lawrence, and selflessly assisted them.

He smiled with asymmetrical, frightening eyes — his grey hair fluffing in a slight movement of the hill breeze.

'One of the many things I know nothing about is falconry. You must explain it to me.'

'It would take six months.'

'Then tell me about the ones you had.'

He was always able to give me a feeling of pleasure and importance.

'Oh, Bunny, don't ask. If I start talking about hawks I go on for ever.'

He fixed me with the eye of Balor.

'Very well. The one I started with was a kestrel. It belonged to a friend. You couldn't train it for much, except catching mice. It had a high voice — kee, kee, kee — and its talons were like needles. We loosed it when it was grown up. Then I got involved with two goshawks from Germany — who taught me a lot. They were enormous, short-winged hawks and you flew them from the glove. After them, I had a pair of merlins — absolute darlings. They were tiny creatures, hardly as big as a pigeon. They were half-way between hawks and falcons. They flew from the fist like hawks, but the chase generally went into the sky, like the old-fashioned chase of peregrines after herons. By, they were glorious! I tried to call them Balin and Balan. But they

15

were identical to look at, so I had to give one of them red jesses and the other one black ones. The result was that in the end they got called Red and Black. You fly them at larks. The lark goes straight up, singing, like a helicopter. The merlin swings away in sweeping circles like a spitfire, often in the opposite direction, to gain height. Do you remember the question in *Hamlet*? "Why do you go about to recover the wind of me, as if you would drive me into a toil?" A merlin has to get upwind of the lark and above it. It's a tremendous aerial combat. They go so high that they are just dots. It ends with a downward streak like a meteor, when they both dive. I made a success with the merlins. They taught me twice as much as the goshawks. One of the nice things about merlins is that you have to loose them before the winter. They are the friendliest hawks. You like setting them free. After that I thought I was ready to start on peregrines. I have lost three of them so far — by stupidity. Now we have Cressida and the tiercel.

'Bunny, listen. What I learnt from the merlins was this. May I tell you about it? Am I boring you? It was a sort of illumination — you know, a sort of Pentecost. The atmosphere became phosphorescent when it dawned on me, like finding the Holy Grail.

'You see, with merlins, you loose the young ones in a barn to begin with. You take in their chopped-up food on a board. After a few days they feed in front of you and will even fly down to the board, while you are chopping the food. Then you capture them, and tie them to their perches out of doors on a leash.

'When you take out their food on the board, they still fly towards it. The next step is to offer the food in your hand.

'But, when I did this, they flew in the opposite direction, as if they were terrified. I tried again and again and again and again. I was in despair. Then the Holy Ghost descended. I thought — it was an effort of thought, like giving birth to something — I thought: They associate food with board, not with hand. How can I make my hand like a board? So I held the hand flat, palm downwards, and laid the food on the back of it. They understood instantly, and came.

'You see, in training a hawk — which has an absolutely different brain structure from yours — you are stringing together a series of conditioned reflexes. Food — Board — Flat Hand — Hand — Me. Eventually they must come to the trainer, even when loose, because they associate him with food. But the gaps between the reflexes must not be too wide. They couldn't bridge the gap from board to hand. So I had to put in a half-way step — the flat hand.

'Do you know, training hawks and training setters are the two most fascinating things in the world? You have to control setters at a distance too. A fool in a fog could train retrievers· But setters! But falcons!'

'How did you lose the peregrines?'

'I miscalculated their age when I got them. I put them out to hack too late and they just cleared off. I am only a learner, Bunny. I am terrified about Cressida and the tiercel.'

A few yards away from us, with his back turned, the keeper

Joyce was eating his own sandwiches. He was a noble retainer, one of the old-fashioned kind who believed in being polite to his laird. He was eating separately by his own choice, not by ours. Beside him was the cadge which he carried, with the two peregrines seated on it motionless, extinguished by their hoods.

'The terrifying thing about Cressida is that sooner or later she is going to have to "wait on". You don't fly peregrines from the glove. You just throw them away into the air, and they go up and up. Five hundred feet, perhaps? Quite loose. Then they circle above you, almost out of sight, and you go forward with the setter, searching for a pack of grouse. When you find a pack, you put them up, and the peregrine dives like a thunderbolt.

'The trouble is, Cressida had her first training with a friend of mine. I have not had her from the beginning. I don't know her properly. But the dreadful moment has to come when I toss her away, with no quarry in sight, and leave her to climb to heaven. Suppose she is not ready to wait-on? Suppose she just clears off like those three eyasses? Suppose it takes us a long time to find a pack of grouse, and she gets bored, and goes? That's why I have been fiddling about all morning, carrying her on the cadge, looking for a good set. If only Brownie would give us a firm point, I would throw her off, wait till she was up, and spring the birds. But Brownie is being wild today, as you saw. She's running in. I daren't trust Cressida to hang about the sky. I don't know what to do. When you have lost three eyasses, it is apt to shake your nerve.'

'Well, what's the answer?'

'Oh, God! I wonder if I could try flying her from the fist? I shall have to think up something. Suppose I carried her like a merlin, with the hood off, and then, if Brownie runs in on the set, I could let her try to overtake from ground level? What do you think?'

'I don't know anything about it.'

'God!'

I put my head in my hands and stared between my knees at a small carnivorous plant, which catches flies on the mountain bog and digests them.

Cressida was a peregrine falcon, at least two years old, who had been trained by one of the greatest of falconers. This gentleman was breaking up his family of hawks and dogs, and had given her to me. She was a crafty old devil, with a distinct character of her own — partly ill-tempered, partly pussy-like if in a good humour, and at times you could almost swear that she had a distorted sense of fun. The trouble was that I did not understand her. I had no means of knowing how thoroughly she had been trained, and she had been spending the winter and spring without work. She had been on holiday in the mews. This was her first day's work for me on a war footing, and I did not know how much she remembered of her previous education. I did not know how much she accepted my control, or whether she was rightly in condition to fly. In any case I was an ignoramus about peregrines.

Falconry is not a hobby or an amusement: it is a rage. You eat it and drink it, sleep it and think it. You tremble to write of it, even in recollection. It is, as King James the First remarked, an extreme stirrer up of passions. Every falconer who reads this book will write angry and contemptuous letters to me, calculated to laud his own abilities and to decry mine. It will be cruelly reviewed in an exclusive little magazine called *The Falconer*, by somebody who has scarcely troubled to read it — if he can read — but who wishes to establish that he is a better falconer than I am — not a difficult thing to establish. In the review, each of my mistakes, which I have carefully pointed out, will be as carefully and tauntingly brought to my attention. So I had better explain at once that what I was going to do was ridiculous.

I ought to have waited till I was sure that Cressida remembered her training and was sharp-set. I ought to have let the setter settle down for a day or two, until I could rely on a steady point. She was a young bitch. Then, on a firm set, I ought to have cast her off until she had reached her altitude, put up the birds as quickly as possible, and enjoyed our triumph.

But I was a learner and no pundit. I had been shaken by the recent loss of the eyasses. I had only been successful with merlins, so I tried to fly her like a merlin. I am not boasting about this, kind falconers, I am confessing it.

'Let's go.'
We moved up wind in the roasting sunshine, stumbling,

sweating, angry and bothered, on the tussocky hill. I took off Cressida's hood, and she was as pettish as we were. She was perfectly trained, though I had no means of knowing it. She expected to be thrown off as usual. Instead, she was held to the glove by her jesses, which she could not understand. She bated in the hot air, panting with rage, her beak open, frowning upon me with her burnt-umber eye.

The humans began to quarrel among themselves, upbraiding each other on assorted topics. We accused each other of going too fast, or going too slow, or being clumsy, or annoying the hawk, or forgetting where the wind was, or anything else which proved handy. The setter, as wild as everybody else, quartered in front of us, out of contact. She had already sent away three packs of grouse that morning, by running in before we could catch up with her. She had also chased a hare. It was the kind of day on which peppery colonels will shout at dogs and thrash them and dance up and down on the mountainside, shaking their fists at heaven. Sometimes, if the dog is far enough away, they discharge their guns upon it.

We were scarcely a mile from Fraoch when Brownie got her set.

She held it.

We hurried.

She was hundreds of yards ahead. She looked over her shoulder at us. I began fatally to yell, 'Steady, steady!' Cressida recognized the point and wanted to take the air, but I checked her. She bated in fury.

Brownie looked over her shoulder a second time, and took one pace.

'Steady, steady!'

She began to snake forward, low to the ground, head and tail in a straight line, slowly, then less slowly, then faster. 'Steady, steady!' Encouraged by the uproar and stampede behind her, she dashed in.

They were off, flickering and whickering, close to the heather.

Cressida flew, half checked by me in a last second of indecision, stumbled in the air and was away. Perhaps they had a hundred yards start of her. She had no altitude and was out of training, because of her long holiday and moult.

Everybody seemed to be running or flying or barking or cursing as the grouse vanished in the distance.

And Cressida, defeated, threw up into the cobalt sky.

I swung the lure round and round my head at intervals till sunset. I blew the whistle. I went over in my mind all the things I ought to have done or ought not to have done. I sulked, with my tail between my legs, and could not encounter Bunny's eye. I tried to invent reasons why it was his fault, or Joyce's, or the dog's. There was nothing to be seen of Cressida — nothing in the wide world.

Before we went to dinner, I left some meat tied to the falcon's block, in case she should grow hungry and come home for it. I also constructed a special trap out of feathers and fishing line, which I had once before used successfully on her. It was not her first escape.

Dinner was a gloomy meal, though everybody tried to talk of something else. Bunny and Ray and their two children were experts at not blaming people for mischances, and they were also sensitive to feelings.

The sun set behind Slieve Fyagh, and a bright star lit itself beyond the shoulder of Corslieve, before I went bitterly to bed.

In the morning, the meat which was tied to the block had not been touched. The tiercel sat on his own block, alone, sometimes cocking his head sideways to gaze at the sky — a fact which I ought to have noticed. Everything felt loose or abandoned, like a tug-of-war in which the other team has let go the rope. I wandered about the garden after breakfast, feeling pointless.

But there must have been something at the back of my mind — an unconscious recollection of a trick I had once read about. I did not remember the trick consciously until I had played it. It developed by itself.

'Well, Joyce, we've lost her. We had better go and shoot some grouse for dinner. In any case, I want Brownie to settle down. Mr Garnett says he is going to try the river.'

'Very good, sir.'

Brownie had been wild because we were wild — anxiety is catching — and because she was confused by the falcons. She had been asked to work with no guns visible — which had muddled her — and it was the beginning of the season, and she was young, and Fraoch was a new place. Now that we were carrying guns instead of hawks and the place was more familiar, she began to behave. She found us a nice set in the flat bog below the Lodge and held it.

We caught up with her, gently patting the rigid rump to urge it very slowly forward, pace by pace. The birds did not want to fly — and I ought to have noticed that too. Trembling, on tiptoe almost, the tail straight and one front paw in the air, she crept with us right among them.

Then they were off. At the first bang, she dropped like a veteran. I chose the second bird and massacred that too.

Is it possible — for it seems so in retrospect — that Cressida struck the second bird before it touched the ground?

When a peregrine stoops from her pitch, you can actually hear the wind in her feathers — a sort of FFFFRP as she hurtles by. When she strikes a flying grouse, she bowls it over in a cloud of feathers, head over heels, exactly as if it had been shot. You can hear the thump. Then she sweeps upward in a stall turn and binds to the body.

So there she was — my beautiful, my crazy Cressida — clutching the dead bird in the heather and glaring at us with an expression I could not decypher. She mantled over the quarry, shielding it with greedy wings as if to keep us away. She began to pluck and toss away the feathers, starting at the head — for she had been superbly educated by the falconer who gave her to me, Gilbert Blaine. A peregrine is allowed the head for a reward, but the body goes to the kitchen.

The Bog

I began to tremble like Brownie. I motioned to Joyce, to stay where he was and hold the bitch.

It was important not to approach too quickly. I waited till she was well into the brains and settling down to them. Then I walked to her slowly, rather circuitously, stood for a few moments, squatted, held out my glove. I lifted her, grouse and all — she not making the faintest protest — and with agonized fingers felt for the jesses which, once held, would bring her into my possession once again.

Joyce and I sighed simultaneously, deeply. I straightened up. We smiled warmly upon one another. God was in his heaven and all was right with the world.

She had been there since we started — out of human sight in the dazzling sky above our heads and beautifully waiting-on. I remembered at last that this was a recognized way of reclaiming a lost falcon — to shoot a grouse for her, in case she was in the offing.

Joyce and I began talking quickly, both at once, telling each other all about it.

We detached the carcase from her talons when she had eaten the head, praising her and helping her to feed meanwhile. It was odd to see that the heather tops in the dead bird's crop were new and undigested.

Joyce collected the other bird and brought it back, after patting Brownie very much. He showed me something which I had not known before — that you can tell the age of a grouse by letting its weight hang from the lower jaw. If it is a young bird, the beak will break.

That evening, after the roast grouse and beautiful claret, with the same star beaming over Corslieve and the cairn of dead King David, I wrote these verses.

This sooty grouse, yet tawny and touched with red,
Weighs handsome on my hand, although he's dead.
One wing reflects the sky. A steely light
Gleams from the primaries he oiled last night,
The twelve bright swords on which he wove his flight.
His crop of heather, which my falcon split
In footing him, spills on my hand. Each bit
Is cleaner than cook's salad, fresh and green
With lilac buds surprising to be seen.
Such was his simple craft, to snip all day and seek
His livelihood of leaves with agricultural beak.

Joyce says: 'An old cock?' But some tint I see,
Reminding me of youth, I disagree.
'I think he's this year's bird.' Joyce takes him, dumb,
Opens the bleeding beak, inserts a thumb,
And weighs him by the lower jaw — which breaks.
'Quite right: this year's.' 'Why so?' 'Well, sir, it takes
An old bird to stand this. He's got more pate.
The young bird's jaw will break with his own weight.'

LOSING A FALCON

How did Man find this out? Who first took heart
To lift his grouse by that unlikely part
And go on lifting till he learned the art?
Seeing how stupid Man is, it's unnerving
To think how long he must have been observing.

IN this village, on the west coast of
Ireland, the population was about
five hundred. There were two hotels.
I stayed at the small one. So did the
school-mistress, Miss Keily, and the representative of the
Land Commission. We had our meals at the same table in
the dining-room, with occasional transients who were passing
through. There were the Hen Woman, a few commercial travel-
lers, and the usual Inspectors of this and that. Tea-time was
about six o'clock.

29

One evening in the middle of July, I walked down the passage to the dining-room, thinking about two things at the same time. One was, the relationship between Sir Launcelot and Queen Guinever: the other was, whether the slight rain of that morning would have brought enough water into the river, where I had a stretch of salmon fishing. It is possible to think about two things at the same time, as it is possible to love two women at the same time, and I was absorbed in both topics as I turned the chromium-plated handle in the door, which was painted to represent the grain of deal.

I went into the room, and, for one half of a heartbeat, the world stood still. I stood — I saw myself from outside, standing — with the door knob in my right hand, my left or advancing foot two inches from the floor, my eyes widening and my mouth open. Then I shut my mouth, narrowed my eyes, put down my foot, closed the door with an effort and advanced as graciously as possible upon the tea-table. I was determined not to seem discourteous.

For there, at the snow-white linen table cloth, vis-à-vis with Miss Keily, who sat spell-bound, like a rabbit confronting a rattle-snake, at tea-time in Eire, in the parish nearest to America, there sat and jauntily conversed a coal-black cannibal.

If only I could give you the impact of him, in that humdrum, customary hotel: of his sharp teeth, actually filed to points, and of his pink, parrot tongue, munching lettuce: of his retreating conical forehead capped with fuzzy hair like black sheepskin

cut close: of the thick, ebon back of his neck, like a motor tyre:
of his small eyes, like a pig's, but toffee-coloured and only able
to meet the European eye up to a certain point. Like a dog he
did not face you eye-to-eye for long. His nose suddenly gave
up the effort to have a bony shape. It curled over at the end in
a fat blob which hid the nostrils, and sank down resignedly upon
the upper lip, as if it were a black wax nose which had been
left out in the sun. Then there were his great shooting simian
lips, only much plumper than an ape's — and the scar on his
right cheek — and the tattoo scars on his temples, giving him
such a savage look — and his long, dark, shiny fingers, pink
inside — and his very good taste in dress, which recognized that
sultry blues with a touch of chocolate, in the shirt and tie,
were the becoming colours for a Moor. His beautiful, bony,
well-built body was over six feet two inches in height (he told
me later) and he weighed 174 pounds. His wrist-watch covered
a scar on the left wrist, inside, but it was difficult to be sure,
on the dark skin, whether it was a scar or some horribly greasy
patch — which it certainly was not. There was a huge single
glass diamond in his gold ring. He was utterly, Nigerianly black.
He was not a brown man, or a coloured man, or a crooner. He
was absolutely a *sable* savage, a strong, bony, black, cannibal
negro. And there he munched away at his lettuce, voraciously,
so that we felt that he might suddenly lean across the tea-table
and plunge his fork into Miss Keily, and gobble her up with
bold, sinuous, strange movements of his blueish lips, and savour
her trotters with circular turns of his small, round-ended,

repellent, pink tongue. Looking into his mouth was like having a private view of somebody's intestines.

It was our Fair Day in the village, and that was why he was there. He was some sort of quack or witch-doctor or racing tipster, like the people you see at horse races, crying, 'I have a horse!' He sold patent medicine.

I sat down meekly before him, noting at the same time that Miss Kelly was about to faint.

Mr Montgomery-Majoribanks — for that was his name — summed me up in a flash. Before you could say Jack Robinson — or, better still, Man Friday — he was off again with a phony Oxford accent, which he put on for my benefit. The accent was just on the Music-Hall side of Public-School. He had guessed that I would be interested in doctors, and had noted the red setter which entered the eating-room at my heels. He gabbled away in this Old-School-Tie voice, about materia medica and nature cures and how he was madly fond of dogs — for which he obviously had a supreme, savage contempt. He told us how he had paid fabulous sums to a vet, to keep one of his dogs alive: and how he kept Alsatians — a whole kennel of them — all of the utmost pedigree and all doted upon. ('Dogs?' Miss Keily must have thought, 'to eat?' At this point she fled the room.)

Then there was the handshake with which we parted after tea. Mr Montgomery-Majoribanks just perceptibly hesitated to offer me his hand: which I thereupon seized emphatically, determined not to be a sahib, curling my palm round his collection of chocolate-pink fingers with a sort of electric shock, and letting go with relief.

I drove out in the Jaguar, to see about the salmon water.

Looking back on him after many years, it was the setting of that Blackymor which made him such a vivid figure — the incongruous setting of the West. For now, as I flogged the unyielding river in the late afternoon, I was in the centre of the desolate Irish scene.

The river, shallow with summer, rippled in herring-bone patterns, like the roof of your mouth, the colour of weak beer, cutting its winding way six feet below the level of the bog. And the bog stretched flat for miles and miles, a landscape out of Browning's *Childe Roland*. Round the rim of the saucer, there were the mountains, as bare, calm and empty as the bog. Perhaps all beauty is melancholy. It seems sad to be lovely.

There were half a dozen cottages along the miles of river, and one abandoned shooting-lodge. The cottages were two-roomed blocks of white-washed material, thatched. The thatch was held down by straw ropes with rocks tied to them. In these, there was a population of old people and grandchildren. Nobody seemed to be middle-aged.

The cottagers took an interest in me. They were kind, and spoke English very well, although their natural speech was Gaelic. Mrs Neary knitted long stockings to go under my waders, with wool from her own sheep, spun on her own wheel, warm and waterproof with the natural lanolin still in them, and

shamefully cheap. Paddy Barrett, who was getting on for eighty
and bent into a hoop with rheumatism, would hobble down to
discuss world politics. Dennis Burke, who was only seventy
and not quite so stiff, had elected himself to be my unpaid
ghillie. He was a volatile, wizened, bird-like, scarecrow figure,
with a wide sense of wonder and curiosity — who had begun
by calling me Your Honour, but soon got over it. We were a
source of interest and surprise to one another. For instance, at
one time I bargained to rent the empty shooting-lodge, of which
he was the caretaker. In this bargain, I ignorantly offered three
times its real value — while at the same time vehemently asserting that I would not pay a penny more — a situation which
baffled him. On the rare times when we hooked a fish, he would
leap about behind me, crying 'Take yer time, now', 'Don't stir'
— all the while taking no time himself, and stirring like mad, as
he hopped on his stiff leg.

It was he who sang, and later wrote laboriously for me in his
own hand, the following song about the island of Inniskea:

SONG CALLED THE PRIDE OF INNISKEA

One Evening fine,
I did incline
To leave my native home
To iniskea

I took my way,
I carelessly did roam.

THE BLACKYMOR

She was modest mild,
loving and kind,
She is the Pride of iniskea.

I quickly steped up to her,
and saluted this fair maid.
Said I my dear
What brought you here,
I Pray from whence you came,
or was it Cupid,
Sent you here,
with his swords so bright this day?
I am in despair,
for you my dear,
Sweet Pride of iniskea.

She quickly made an Answer,
Saying young Man don't me annoy,
for I am but A simple maid,
therefore Pass me by,
my father is A Fisherman,
and he is away at Sea,
my dwelling Place,
lies but A space,
so young man, go your way.

THE BLACKYMOR

Said I my Pretty fair maid,
I hope you will me excuse,
As you are A fisherman's daughter,
Oh do not me refuse,
I am A wealthy farmer,
I came bathing to the sea,
and when my month is over,
with me you'll come away.

and if it's to the sea you came,
young man where are your pains,
or are you Parilised she said,
or are you blind or lame?
if you have Patience Kind sir,
she said,
yonder lies the main,
and you may swim there like a Duck,
and it will cure you of your Pain.

all the water in that sea,
from here to Achill Sound,
would not cure me of my Pains,
or heal me of my wounds,
since I have seen your loving face,
from you I cannot go,
I live near Crossmolina town,
in the County of Mayo.

Kind sir
you might be A foreigner,
that came here for to bathe,
although you do pertend to me
Your riches it is Great,
I'd rather have A fisherman
that would Sail and Plough the Sea,
and rowell me on his arms
when crossing over the deep.

Farewell, farewell
to iniskea,
as now my month is over,
although I came to Cure my pains,
I am worse A Great dale more,
if I could Gain that lovely maid
so Beautiful and fair,
its forever I'd live Content,
with my love in Ineskea.

Another of Dennis Burke's accomplishments was to tell stories about local history. One of his best stories went like this: 'In Kildun there is a stone, marked with a cross, which is said to cover the resting place of the Giant of Kildun. This giant was shaving one day, and had the half of his face shaved, when a white hare burst into his dwelling and ran about. It leaped up into his arms, and he clutched it, and surveyed it. Then it ran out of the door and made off in the direction of the Fort of Drumgollagh. At this fort there lived another giant, a friend of the giant's at Kildun. The shaving giant, laying down his razor, determined to follow the magic hare, and did so. It led him to Drumgollagh, where the giant of that place, his friend, told him to leave off chasing the hare, because he claimed it for himself. At this, the two giants had high words. Each said that he was as good a man as the other, and was as much entitled to the hare as he was, and finally they fell to fighting. The giant of Kildun hit the giant of Drumgollagh upon the forehead and made him dead. Then he returned to his home in Kildun, a broken man, *finished shaving*, and committed suicide from the remorse that was at him.'

It was Dennis Burke also, this elderly, bright, jerky, patched rag-bag of a bard, who told me the features of the river. He shewed me the Mass Pool, beside which, in the old days of persecution, the Catholic peasants used to come for their worship. He shewed the ruins of the church of Tean, which had been built by St Tean, with the aid of some religious sheep. They carried the stones for him.

In return for his entertainment and instruction, I did my best for the rheumatism of Dennis and Paddy, bringing them celery pills and Fynnon's salt and other nostrums.

So now, with our cannibal in the offing, I began to have one of my schemes. Whatever his qualifications as a doctor, the black man had claimed that he was, and had shewn himself by his conversation to be, an enthusiastic masseur. Perhaps they might have perfected some massage of their own, in the hinterlands of Nigeria?

I confided to my two friends that I would try to bring Mr Montgomery-Majoribanks with me, to treat their aching joints next evening. Paddy, in his old, beautiful, soft, assuring voice, said that I was a kind man. He said 'kind' kindly. Dennis became excited.

When it was time to reel in and leave the river, with nothing caught, Dennis said angrily to the fishes something like 'Marbh faiscithe ar an iasc' — a death tightening on the fish. Perhaps he referred to the band with which they tie up a corpse's chin. He was cross with them for not having been caught.

I packed up and left the heart of Ireland for the heart of Africa.

On the second day of the Fair, Mr Montgomery-Majoribanks turned up to tea once more, and we were alone. He said that he had had a 'disastrous' day. (Probably he had had a good one.) But he looked tired, and was quieter. He did not lecture about medicine and manipulation, but now accepted me as an intellectual equal. I began to feel a warmth for him — though it was still a strange feeling. He only told two lies, and he dropped the Music-Hall accent. I asked about the colour bar.

He said stoically that he 'could take it'. He took no notice of the sahib business, he said, as he was tough enough to ignore it, and 'had good nerves'. All human beings were horrible, he thought, and one form of horribleness was much the same as another. So he took the horrors of the white men philosophically. (I was surprised to notice that he was talking like a grown-up.) Questioned about his present life — it did not seem right to probe the pre-civilized era of his tattoo marks, for his attitude had made it plain that he did not want to be seen in that light — he told me that he had been 'trained' in England, 'practised' in various parts, 'choosing the place carefully, to avoid prejudice'. He told how he had been in Ireland for four years and had a big round — how he had been run out of some place by the local talent — how he had insured his massaging hands for £25,000. (He was as poor as a church mouse, of course, and could not have insured them for anything. Or could he — as a kind of panacea, as a kind of gesture to keep his courage up, like the glass diamond ring?) He told how he now toured the country from fair to fair, selling medicine. He intended to set up a practice in Cork, and had just come from there, a terrible journey, in one day, by car, to be at our tiny festival. Then he rambled on a bit about dogs and his love for them, to please me. He observed at last that he had 'always kept himself neat and decent'.

It dawned on me then what a splendid fellow he was, this lone savage so bold in the civilized jungle. He was infinitely poor, bearing up against the unrelenting stares and hostility, keeping himself 'neat and decent' in his fighting colours of blue and chocolate. He only had one suit, which he sponged and cleaned every night. He was not welcome in hotels. They would not give him sheets, believing his colour to be dirty. I suddenly

saw him in his bare, enemy, empty bedroom, much cleaner than
I was — surgically clean — pressing his one suit under the
mattress, a lone wolf. He did physical jerks, morning and
evening, and banted on vegetables whenever his weight rose
above twelve stone six. He kept himself fit and neat and tried
'to take it'. He had to. Like a white man in the depths of the
jungle, depending upon his fitness, he was a jungle man in the
depths of civilization, a leopard stepping catlike, dainty, through
the traffic of Oxford Circus.

What a noble front to life! How brave! And think of that
nightmare drive from Cork, to collect a few shillings among us.
For, when I shewed him a road map, discussing the best route,
I found that he could not read it. 'Is this all Ireland?' he asked,
looking at a large-scale map of Mayo. Then he read with pleasure
the name of a bay. 'Blacksod!' he exclaimed with delight.

'Don't you get very tired,' I asked, 'driving from fair to fair
like this?'

'I have Good Nerves. I can Take It.'

'But all those people standing round you this afternoon, and
staring like cattle, while you shouted and lectured. Doesn't all
that lecturing exhaust you?'

'I only lecture for half an hour. Then I sit in the car and have
a cigarette. I try to sell them bottles. Then I lecture again.'

I had a vivid picture of his passionate bawling, waving his
arms like a tipster, in the dirty, dung-spattered market place,
among the scared, drivelling bullocks, and I said again: 'Well,
I would not be able to keep it up.'

41

He suddenly admitted comically: 'It is dreadful. Nobody goes to fairs to buy medicine. They go to enjoy themselves, and they don't want medicine a bit. I have to *make* them want it.'

'What a wicked profession!'

'It's *diabolical*,' he said, with satisfaction. 'I take strong, healthy men, and make them feel ill, and then I sell them a bottle!'

'Don't you get mixed up in a lot of fights? I mean, everybody is always drunk at fairs, and ...'

But I did not like to mention the tipsy white people, wanting to mob him because he was not white.

'I am a Tiger in the North,' he said proudly. 'We have better facilities in the North.'

Then, more proudly: 'If a drunk man hits me there, I let him have it. And the police will protect you. But here, in the South, the guards can't protect you. So I can't hit back here.'

How valiant these fellows must be, I thought — the Indians and others who circulate through Europe — explorers in a strange, hostile, dangerous forest of civilization, far more dangerous than the Amazon, selling us cheap rugs, living on a bit of rice, risking their bronze-skinned lungs in fogs not understood. What Livingstones and Stanleys meet in Whitechapel I wonder?

Reflecting on the subject of drink, he confided that only two bottles of stout would make him 'stinking' drunk — there came a strong revulsion in my mind when he used this adjective —

but he said that when he was drunk he was not quarrelsome, only very sleepy.

He agreed to visit our patients in the evening, and he questioned me shrewdly enough about their age and about how long they had had their rheumatics. Obviously he had little hope of doing anything for them.

'Will they keep to a diet?'

'No, of course not. They can't afford to have diets. They have to eat what they have. But you might relieve them for the moment, and cheer them up.'

He insisted that I should go with him, either fearing to lose his way or else being bashful. Bashful? That warrior? Well, yes, It was the barrier about his colour — faced dauntlessly but it was there. He was an energetic, enthusiastic, athletic, brave, simple and honest charlatan, and he was sensitive. I never asked how old he was. He was in the prime of life, probably about thirty.

I went across the road to the Garage, to ask Jack whether he wanted to come. There were two businessmen from Dublin with him, something to do with motor cars, who were on their way back from a holiday in Donegal. They wanted to come too. They said it would be 'something not to miss', to see the darkie massaging the simple crofters. This made me feel uncomfortable, for I had not been meaning any kind of joke. I wanted to give Mr Montgomery-Majoribanks a chance of earning a little money, and to pay my friends Dennis and Paddy a delicate attention. However, the subtle Dublin mind saw it as an elaborate trap or hoax or lampoon, which made me unhappy.

There were the usual troubles about getting our party en route. Its members kept breaking off to have tea, or another drink, or to fetch something. It was getting on for evening. The Guardai had already dispersed three fair-day fights in the main street — though it was too early yet for the baton charge. At last we managed to fix it that the masseur should go in his own car with Jack, while I followed in their car with the Dubliners, taking rods in case we wanted to fish afterwards. At the last moment a drunk sea-fisherman from the islands saluted me. 'Conas ta tu?' 'Ta me go mait, go raibh mile mait agat.' 'How are you?' he wanted to know. 'I am doing fine, thank you very much.' What sort of weather was it going to be, we asked each other. He wanted to talk, to share the warmth of his heart. He threw his arms round my neck, saying that he had heard I was a Russian, and, as for him, he would rather have the Russians here than the English. This was to flatter me, on the supposition that I might be a Russian, and partly to find out if I was. I mentioned that it would be better not to have either. He agreed, readily, but reverted to his previous proposition. He was a large, whiskery man. I pacified him at last and escaped — while he staggered off to wait for the baton charge, satisfied as to my nationality. It was now eight o'clock.

Great was the welcome which waited us at the home of Dennis, who had given us up and was dressed in his working clothes. For that matter, he had never really expected us. There was such a lot of blarney in Eire that people put little reliance on each other's word, and did not fret about disappointments.

We stepped into the stone-floored room of the cottage, with its built-in bed and black chimney, holding a turf fire. Mysterious articles hung from the rafters of the roof. There was a gramophone with a tin horn. Everybody dashed about shyly. Neighbours began to arrive to share the excitement. The gramophone was started, and a little girl of three or four began to dance. She hopped or shuffled gravely round and round, her bare feet whispering on the wet floor, her gaze fixed upon us, not very much in time with the metal music.

Jack called her to him. 'Here is a present for you. Open your hand and let me put it in.' But she held the cold paw tight shut, staring with big, expressionless eyes. 'Don't be afraid now.' 'Sweets,' said Dennis's sister. So the paw opened, and sixpence was put in.

Chickens, nephews and others entered. A boy was sent to fetch old Paddy from the other side of the river — kind Jack volunteering to carry the old man over. The Dubliners and I sat in a row by the window, conversing with the company, admiring the pot-hook and the strong tea in a metal pot at the fire, with its rusty ashes. Mr Montgomery-Majoribanks, a towering, ebon figure, stood proudly in the background, silent, important, professionally reserved. All agreed that Dennis would soon be supple.

It was an impressive moment when he was laid upon the bed,

chirping, protesting feebly as his trousers were taken down. And impressive it was too, in the lamplight and the gathering dusk, as the huge, double-jointed, umbrageous fingers seized him by the ankles and twisted and yanked his knotted white legs in every possible direction, and spanked and chopped and rubbed his stomach and his spine, in deadly serious taciturnity. Every eye was fixed upon the scene, the hush broken only by the squeaks, remarks and muffled exclamations of the patient. ('Sure, I could jump me own heighth wance. Ow!') Excitement grew as the limbs began to seem more elastic. The fingers

Massaging the patient

46

kneaded into him, probing into the roots of his bones. Jack came over the river with ancient Paddy pick-a-back, entered ('Good avening, ma'am'), and set him down. The eighty-year-old gentleman, small, gentle, pleased, impressed, watched the final stages of the operation, shrunk into himself. It was evident that every angle of Dennis was bending and folding better than it had done for twenty years.

The maestro paused, relented. He was enjoying himself tremendously, showing off. There was no patter now, no fair-ground spieling, but only a genuine manipulator — he was really good — soaking his ego in the admiration which I was happy to lend him. He was play-acting for me to the top of his bent, being mysterious, monosyllabic, withdrawn. He was bubbling inside, wanting to shout with pleasure at himself, but the act was lofty grandeur — Sir James Montgomery-Majoribanks, the eminent surgeon! Well, he had been kicked round Ireland as a quack for four years, so it was high time that somebody loved him.

The eminent surgeon did me the honour of calling me into consultation.

We withdrew to a corner of the room and whispered. The trouble was deep seated, he said. He could do nothing more without his lamp. (It was one of those round, copper, electric radiators, and he had it in the car.) I mentioned to my leader that the cottage was not wired for electricity, but he fetched the radiator all the same. It was obvious that he was longing to get at Dennis with it while he was still supple. He was succeeding, and he wanted to do a good job. It was also obvious that he did not understand about electricity. The lamp was like the maps to him. He held it in loving reverence. It was his fetish.

Everybody began to discuss the whereabouts of the nearest electricity, and whether the two old gentlemen would feel it worth while, so late at night, to be driven the ten miles to our hotel, where we knew there was some. The atmosphere had to be tested cautiously. If we had suggested that they ought to come, they would have done so out of politeness. It was important to be allusive, sensitive, tangential, important not to suggest anything. We wagged our antennae at each other with delicate inquiry, like ants meeting. Eventually it turned out that they did want to come. Dennis was awe-struck by the fact that he could bend his stiff knee at last. Both were fervent patients and believers already, and they had been holding back only for fear that they might be a nuisance to the gentry.

So it was decided that the Blackymor should drive them to the village and back again, for their electric treatment, while we, the anglers, went off to fish at the Pool of Peace.

If it seems odd that we should go fishing at this time of night, it has to be remembered that it was Fair Day. We had taken a couple of bottles of Jameson to entertain the neighbourhood, being determined to do some good to the patients, one way or another, and the bottles were now empty.

The Pool of Peace, an inlet of the sea, communicated with the Main through a narrow race. The passage flowed at a

tremendous rate of knots, and the right moment for the big
sea-trout was at the turn of the tide. There was a ferry, operated
by a wild Gaelic family called McMennamin — who had some
sort of fishing rights with a salmon net, and who used to
provide us, if warned, with sand-eels for bait.

But it was late, and we had not warned them, and the family
themselves were hauling on their net. We flogged away with the
wet fly for a while, in the turmoiling water, and the summer
twilight drew in with rain and mist, as the salmon and sea-trout
jumped with surprising plops that raised a fever in the blood.
Then we went over to watch the men at the net.

This inlet was many miles from the home of Dennis, and we
had no rights in it. Who had? The sporting rights of Eire were
claimed by proprietors of the richer classes, but denied by the
locals. Since prehistory, the rights of hunting had been common
to all. You paid for them or did not pay for them in proportion
as you were locally accepted. Jack and I were more or less
accepted, and had never paid, and did not know whom to pay.
It was enough to tip the McMennamins for the sand-eels, or to
hire their boat. Now some message or other had been left for us
by a distant water bailiff, saying naughtily that we were to hand
over five shillings or give our names. We all stood about in the
drizzle, plunged once more in the sensitive, receptive, interro-
gative reserve of Irish silence, our antennae rigid. Ought we to
pay or was this bailiff cheating us and what exactly was the
intrigue? Being in Eire was rather like being married. You had
to concentrate and be wide awake, to recognize what the lady

meant. Can you have rights in tidal water? Who, if so, was actually the absent proprietor? Were we local or were we gentry? What prehistoric brehon law was the one which did in fact prevail? We pondered severally, while the foreman of the net, who had delivered the message half in Gaelic, stood non-committally by, with a soft kind of laissez-faire or laissez sentir.

The net came shorewards the last few yards, and the still scene exploded into action. The taut, brown, sinewy, speechless, taciturn haulers burst into a wild hilarity of barbarism, leaped in among the slashing, arching, silver bodies, grabbed them and bashed them savagely with bits of wood, clumsily, hitting the wrong places, shouting, grinning, ferocious, hysterical, more Italian than anything north of Sicily.

There were eleven salmon.

Then there was the long drive home in the pouring dark, with more whisky discovered in the boot of the car. There was the village street abandoned to the aftermath of the Fair, cow-pats and tattered paper and broken wands for beating the cattle, gleaming in the headlights and the rain. The Blackymor's car stood empty outside the hotel. The annual baton charge was over, and it was midnight.

Jack invited us in, and produced a crate of Guinness. Our faces glowing with liquor, our eyes more flashing, our tongues volubly tripping and repeating, we had great concert of talk and narrative, admiring ourselves and one another with warm, welcoming, smiling, appreciative, comradely, rosy hearts. We talked of motor engines and Henry Ford, of poithín and the fairy fire, of famous poachers and deeds of blood and all the subtle stratagems of the Gael.

At 2 a.m. I went across the road to bed. I was feeling tired now, and pettish. That attempt to extract five shillings from us at the race! Everybody swindled me all the time, I thought, and all the people I tried to help ended by stinging me. The Blackymore had driven at least forty miles on his errands of mercy, had seriously improved the patients, and would have to be paid. He was leaving next morning — or rather this one. I sat down and wrote him a note, enclosing two pound notes: 'Dear Mr Montgomery-Majoribanks, I hope this will be all right? Yours sincerely.' Well, he would be certain to kick up a shindy about it, to claim that his usual fee was five guineas, to clamour for more — the eternal parasitic avaricious treacherous beggary which was everywhere in Ireland! Besides, he was a quack, a trickster. He would know that I was soft, and would behave like all the other predators in the jungle of civilization, who seek their prey. He would have me routed out of bed at an early hour, to create a scene. But I was feeling drunk, and wanted a long sleep.

Our landlady was still up. I gave her the envelope.

'Mrs Corduff, please give this to the blackymor. It's his fee. He's bound to ask for more, but *make* him take it. *Don't* wake me up. Just make him take it and *go away*. You see?'

So I was wrong as usual.

In the morning, there was a neat note on the breakfast table. It said:

Dear Mr White

      Many thanks for enclosed fee, but honestly I did not expect so much being we are friends.

Sincerely yours,
James Montgomery-Majoribanks

I suddenly felt happy about him, and also about the sufferers. Even if it did no permanent good to their rheumatism, perhaps it was good for their spirits. It gave them something to think about in the boundless bog, gave them mental fuel. It had made them for a brief space the centre of interest and importance. It was a change.

NOBODY could say that his had been a successful life. It pointed no moral — unless it was the moral of humility. He must have been one of the few humans who did not go about admiring themselves for being God's greatest product. But, except for the wives he married, his humbleness seems to have made him happy.

There is no medical definition for insanity. Legally speaking, being insane means thinking differently from other people. For us, Einstein is a raving lunatic — while all women are maniacs to all men, and vice versa. Birds often behave as if they were slightly crazy.

Desmond seems to have been right about the world in which he lived. He fitted it. 'You have to wait a long time yet,' he once pondered, summing things up. 'It isn't people at all, it's birds.'

It was Jack of the Garage who told me about him, during one of the long evening visits of talk and stories and Guinness by the generous turf fire — almost a ceilidhe — which often ended our expeditions. Jack and I used to shoot or fish on most Wednesdays and Saturdays, and on Sunday after Mass. Jack was a man of unquenchable optimism. He always hoped that the wind would be right or that the rain would hold off or that there would be enough petrol, or that, whatever the threatened calamity was, it would not happen. This made him a bad guide in practical decisions, for the calamity usually did happen. But it made it impossible not to love him. He was in the prime of life, a middle-sized, smiling man with crow's-feet round his warm eyes, and nut-brown cheeks. His hair was carefully oiled flat, but thinning — his hands often smeared with the dark, metallic products of the garage. His strong and amiable wife was older and richer than himself. They were childless. In some ways he had the kindness and willingness of a spaniel, without its fawning, and the fact that he was lovable was matched by the fact that he loved other people, or perhaps was due to it.

His one obstinacy was a conscious refusal to speak ill. On politics, or English tyranny, or religious differences, or merely on the ill-nature of neighbours, he shut his soft mouth in a hard line and refused to utter.

This hopefulness about his fellow men resulted in his having a wide circle of friends, its radius about twenty miles round the village. They came from all walks of life — such as the walks were in Mayo. His own class was presumably the Middle one. He was the richer kind of shop-keeper and proprietor of the only garage. But a hundred cottages — in a few of which English was scarcely understood and the income of a large family as little as ten shillings a week — had a welcome for him as a friend and equal. He seemed to prefer the peasants to the shop-keepers. On market days, you could be sure of some gnarled, voluble figure in flannel and dark cloth flapping wide, brandishing a drover's stick, embracing Jack, quaffing the best thing that ever came out of Ireland — Irish whisky, which makes people brilliant rather than besotted. They bought it, preferring a brand inferior to the best, at the small bar and grocery which masked the garage and which was attended by his firm wife.

Their house was along the yard, between the bar and the garage. The living-room was solidly furnished with heavy pieces like the mahogany side-board and the gleaming, black-leaded kitchen-range. The pictures of the Pope and of the Sacred Heart were in stout frames. The little, permanent red lamp in front of the latter was a rarity — an electric one, run from the generator in the garage. The massive armchairs and the hard couch were Victorian or Edwardian. It was a house-proud room, rather unusual in Eire, for everything was dusted and polished. Its crowning feature was a fungus.

Goodness knows what it was a fungus of, or whether it was vegetable or mineral. It existed under a glass dome, like the wax fruits of Victoria's day, and it grew, and it had to be fed sometimes on liquids. By colouring these liquids, its own colour could be altered. It was horrible and frightening, a malignant growth like some disease in a bottle from a dissecting room. It was convuluted and cellular like a fossil sponge or the lungs of some dread Martian — filamented, mycelian, sporous. It was vividly, odiously coloured with electric blues, arsenical greens, evil violets and sick-room pinks. It had a personality. It was proudly and solicitously tended by Jack's wife. I never saw its like elsewhere.

In this bright, solid, cosy, overcrowded room — one of the few houses in the village with electric light because it made its own — we passed the winter evenings of hospitality. We sat there tired after great winds in the sunset behind stone walls flighting duck, sustained by Guinness or Jameson, presided over by the Thing. Jack was a great narrator, with a relish for character in his stories. He had an enthusiasm for odd people. He drew them out, coaxing them to reveal themselves, noticing and remembering and afterwards being able to reproduce them — always affectionately. He was not that chronic kind of Irish bore — the witty anecdotalist — nor was he the misty, consti-pated bard, with glazed eyes like the younger Yeats, pompously hypnotizing himself with legendary rubbish about the Fianna. He was not self-conscious, and he put on no false acts, It was simply that he enjoyed real people or nice events, and loved to bring them alive by telling about them, and he was good at doing it. His round face would glow with urgency, as he tried to re-create for me this person or that adventure. His wife, usually silent, would sometimes remember a trait and add it to the picture.

One evening, before going to bed, I scribbled a few pencil notes about one of his character-sketches. It was the story of Desmond. Here they are — a hasty and sleepy memorandum just as it was written down. It is not poetical in a humbug way. and has no witty point. It is the ordinary, unedited, not literary conversation, which pours out naturally all over the West of Ireland.

Jack's friend, the old peasant who thinks he is 'in the bird life'. He is 75.

Every Christmas he came to the village for his annual gift of drink, tobacco and matches from Jack. He had looked forward to this since ten years. He is bed-ridden now and lies in bed singing like a bird. He has promised Jack entry to 'bird life' and only his bosom friends will he have admitted.

Often has Jack taken him fishing to Kiltean, and in the summer, on homeward trips, the moths have been all about the lights of the car. Then Jack says, 'Look at those things.' 'Don't be afraid,' says he. 'They are looking after you and I, and keeping us company.' Or when Jack and he have gone to preserved waters, he has consoled Jack, saying: 'If anyone molests you, tell me what happened, and I will deal with them very soon.' 'And how would you deal with them, Desmond?' 'I will get those people evicted from their homes, if they're not very careful, because they are not in the bird life.'

He sings now like a parrot in bed, and, when visited by somebody, he says: 'When did you change your clothes?' (this is the moult). 'Hello, hello,' he can say, like a polly.

He sings now like a parrot in bed

He always would watch the birds in the air, and ask: 'Did you ever see me up there, Jack?' Before being bed-ridden he would feed them from his little back kitchen, and, him being a bird himself, he thought they understood him better than a human. Now that he is bed-ridden, he is a caged bird. But, like caged birds, he sings better than ever.

He would never go in a car with anyone, only with Jack. (My peregrines won't let anybody drive except me.)

'I'm expecting 'em tonight.'

'Who?'

'You don't know.'

Great trouble in making him tell. Then he revealed that he was expecting the migration from the South of France.

'I'll be going with them tonight, but I'll be back again in the morning.' The earth-bound, injured bird could fly in dreams. He used to become uneasy at migration times, and would go out to look at the sky. 'Tell me, is he above?' Did he mean God, or the leader of the geese? (Here Jack's wife put in that he would sometimes migrate himself, in actuality, being absent for three or four months. Perhaps he went as a labourer to England? Nobody knew.)

He could become other creatures.

'Jack,' he says to Jack, 'did ye ever see me in the water?'

'No, Desmond, I never did.' 'Well,' he says, 'if you did see, you'd be frightened. Because one day I saw myself in the water and I was so big I was frightened.' (He had seen his reflection and thought he was a fish.) Once, when in old age he was fishing a pool, Jack was afraid he would be drowned, and tried to interfere. 'Jack,' he says, 'you don't know what I can do. If I fell in, I would be out again with a swish.' (The salmon leaping.)

He always got worse at full moon.

He had been twice married to 'the wrong kind of people'. I asked whom? But both were firmly reticent about badness — just 'the wrong kind of people'. He had taken to drink.

On the world:

One day in the sunset, Jack says to him: 'That's a beautiful sunset.' He looked at Jack and laughed. 'That's not a sunset at all,' he said. 'They are lighting,' says he, 'the lamps in Castlebar.' (There is a mental hospital in Castlebar.) 'That's very funny.' 'You don't understand the world at all, because, if ye did, ye'd be terrible frightened. The world is spinning on a big axle, and that axle is suspended from the heavens on a spider's web. There's men oiling that axle day in and day out. And the colours you see, there are men painting all day and night, and they use millions of gallons of paints, painting those paints, and the clouds and everything.'

'And when you die, you won't be dead at all. You'll still be flying around.'

He was thinking of angels.

'You have to wait a long time yet. It's not people at all, it's birds.'

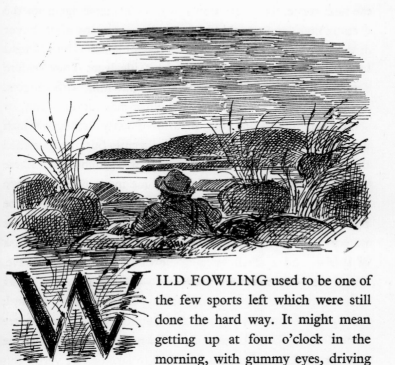

ILD FOWLING used to be one of the few sports left which were still done the hard way. It might mean getting up at four o'clock in the morning, with gummy eyes, driving the car for twenty miles to where you thought the geese were going to cross the coast line, plodding for a couple of miles in winter darkness across the sea-marsh at risk of your life (from the tide), digging yourself a shallow grave in the freezing sand and lying in its icy-harsh water for half an hour or more, like a doll in a cardboard box. Then you saw the lovely battalions pass

61

out of range, drove home for breakfast, and spent the daylight hours spying for the creatures with binoculars, with a view to the next sortie. You went down to the salt-marsh again for the evening flight and possibly had one glass too many after dinner at the inn. Goose-shooters used to resemble the White Knight in *Alice in Wonderland*. They had his idealism. They seldom shot any geese. They were hung about, like him, with gadgets. No goose-man ever went out without a magnum shotgun, or some even more cumbrous firearm of vasty calibre — which went off with a Boom and whose recoil gently but firmly pushed the shooter over backwards, when it was discharged. There were hand-made cartridges for the same in all sizes of shot, a goose-bag into which the dead goose was in theory going to be put — and for sitting on, in the puddles, for it was oiled to be waterproof — a tide-table, a compass, an electric torch, a flask of spirits, and a small kitchen shovel for digging the grave. These were the minimum needs.

It was possible to pursue this fantasy in the West of Ireland, among the boundless bogs of the County Mayo. Geese were more difficult there, because they did not necessarily cross the coast at all. They might fly from bog to lake or vice versa. But there was a rare variety of whitefront at a place which had better not be named. These weighed 25 per cent more than other whitefronts, and, in my opinion, did not migrate. I was mad to shoot some, to weigh them for statistics.

To get the feeling of my story, you will need some picture of the West.

When Cromwell evicted the native Irish from the more
fertile lands, to settle his own adventurers, he told them to get
to Hell or Connaught. Perhaps he did not actually identify Hell
with Connaught. But any Cockney, New Yorker or society
figure would do so, even now. In those days the almost prehistoric settlements were inaccessible by road. There were no
roads. The treacherous parts of the bog, on routes known only
to the inhabitants, like the footpaths of animals, could only be
crossed by throwing down brushwood. The culture of the huge
district was prehistoric — like a La Tène culture of lake dwellings. It is still possible to drive fifteen or twenty miles on a
modern road across the level, russet plain, without seeing more
than a dozen dwellings. Round the great provinces of turf and
heather, whose peat-soil, when wet, is a gleaming roast-coffee
blancmange, the abrupt, lonely mountains make an eternal skyline. On the coast, the anfractuous cliffs are dotted with a series
of promontory forts made long before the dawn of history. The
earth is hospitable only to the potato, the fuchsia and the
rhododendron. A fisherman from Belmullet, so Jack told me,
once walked the endless miles to Ballina. When he saw his first
tree, he fell down and worshipped it.

In winter, this was a hardy, starving territory, a melancholy
steppe. On the few sunny days of summer, it was so beautiful
that your gorge rose in your throat — coming across a lovely
tarn, bluer than the sky, solid cobalt, a secret jewel dropped from
heaven, and bluer than heaven. At sunset, in some atmospheric
conditions, the horizontal rays would for a few moments turn

everything saffron — but everything. The earth, the sky, the turf stacks, the white-washed cottage, all momentarily would glow into glory, like the bars of an electric fire warming up, and the same copper colour.

On this particular evening, in the winter, we drove to the farthest settlement — it could hardly be called a village — at the most isolated fold of the vastest bog there was. It was called in Gaelic, the Cow Bog. Although it was fifteen miles away, Jack as usual knew the people. He was popular with them, and they spoke to him in English, though they spoke their own language among themselves and one or two of the very old ones could speak nothing else. They were as hardy as snipe.

We arrived before darkness, a freezing evening, with the Atlantic wind unchecked by a single perpendicular thing between there and America. There were about half a dozen thatched cottages, with their black turf ricks. There was a kind of track between them.

The people of Shanataggle received us with stately, almost Spanish courtesy. The music-hall caricature of an Irishman as a sort of funny gorilla, with a pig on a string and a clay pipe stuck in his hat — which is fiercely resented by the real Irish — is their own fault. The people of the east coast clowned it like that about a hundred years ago, to diddle the English, and now the picture has stuck to them. But the true Gael was never funny. A spare, gaunt hidalgo of a figure, reserved and sensitive and subtle and wicked in many ways — talkative only when drunk or in emotional release or to mask an anxiety-neurosis by buffoonery — innocently brutal or beautiful by turns. He lives in direct, not artificial, immediate response to circumstances, rightly despising the blunt, uncomprehending codes of the Saxon. There is an intuitive, realistic, *feminine* ferocity in his mind — for women are ruthlessly real. The Gael is a Spaniard, a Malvolio, no comic. For that matter, when the Armada was driven north around the coasts of Scotland, some galleons did come to wreck among the stony fangs of western Ireland. Who can tell what sallow don, escaping massacre, has left his fiery blood among the black-haired, blue-eyed, stately savages of Shanataggle?

They ushered us into the best house and set us down with ceremony to drink strong tea, incomparably brewed in a metal pot with the turf ashes raked round it. The tea had a faint, pleasant tang of peat. It became obvious that there was only one egg in the house. This was presented to me, lightly boiled, with home-baked bread and sweet butter. It would have been churlish not to accept the egg, or to have made even the most allusive attempt to pay for it. If you had given a shilling or two to the smallest child present, under the pretence of making a gift, it would have been identified at once as a trick, an ungentlemanly and obtuse rejection of the hospitality meant by the egg. Also, it would have been churlish not to sit down to the unwanted meal, although the daylight was slipping away and we still had far to walk. Everything in Eire always was late so the best thing was to accept the fact.

A certain amount of nonsense gets written about the hospitality of peasants. The true reason for it, if you face it without being sentimental, is that a stranger is precious to them. The entertainment, the novelty, the something-to-think-about, the mental pabulum, the refreshment of a new ingredient in the cud of one another — which is all they have to chew through winter nights from birth to death — these made me well worth an egg to them. The hospitality was an effort to detain me. Although it may seem that they were conferring something on me, it was I who was really conferring a refill of subject matter for their strong, starved, intelligent minds. I was like a new book to some scholar, marooned away from libraries. This was why it would have been unthinkable not to linger with their egg, submitting to be absorbed.

Jack soon had the flow of talk in motion. He related how, on a previous visit some years since, after a whole bottle of poithín, the octogenarian of the neighbourhood had leapt a ten foot rivulet, his coat-tails flying. This story led to anecdote and speculation, to politics and legend and philology, while every eye watched every motion of the Englishman, a cynosure, to store him up for future nourishment. On the subject of eggs and Gaelic, which I was doing my best to learn, I gleaned for my own interest one piece of information.

It seems that the great Irish pirate-queen Gránia O Mhaille, once attracted the attention of Queen Elizabeth — to whom, incidentally, she tried without success to refuse any form of homage. Gránia's headquarters before capture were at a

tronghold on Clare Island in Clew Bay. Elizabeth, interested
by her savage rival, made inquiries about the Irish and their
ongue. An illustration of the barbaric language was given to
her, thus: 'd'it damh dubh ubh amh ar neamh.' She thought it
sounded very peculiar — not so peculiar, however, as Gránia O
Mhaille considered a similar English sentence: 'Beg a big egg
from Peg.'

A thin boy of about nineteen came in, while we were conversing on subjects of similar interest, and sat down without
speaking in the corner. He was evidently exhausted by his day's
work, and was given a hunk of bread to revive him.

He was a person of startling beauty. He had those lovely,
curved shins — skeletal — which made you long to be a timber
wolf and gnaw them in some den, or an archaeologist to unwrap
them from a mummy. They curved like a Persian bow. His
lengthy, fragile fingers were ducal — no, they were princely.
The blue-black hair fell over sapphire eyes. He was tired,
hungry, so shy in his dignity that I do not think he looked at me
or spoke directly to me the whole evening. He was a Masai
warrior. He should have leaned on a spear in a leopard skin,
drinking bullock's blood, with one leg curled round the other,
his body painted a rusty colour, like the turf ashes. He was the
son of the house, and was to be our guide.

Jack was the merry fellow who got on well with everybody.
The Masai trusted him enough to speak in monosyllables. Such
conversation as he was willing or able to exchange with me had
to be carried on through Jack, as if the latter were an interpreter.

Probably the boy did not understand a word I said, having hypnotized himself into the belief that he would not be able to. (Once, driving into Galway with an Irish speaker next to me in the long Jaguar, we had drawn up beside one of those black-hatted peasants in a bainín, to ask the way. Although spoken to in his own language by a compatriot, he had understood nothing. He had been convinced by the sight of the car that he would not be able to understand.) Besides, with our spearman there was the vaulting ambition and superbity of youth, which made him self-conscious, confused, proud and ashamed, friendly and resentful. He had that struggling look of somebody who is sulking and does not want to sulk, the eyes saying tormentedly, I am stuck in this: please help me out. He was a nobleman in hated chains.

When the decencies had been observed, I managed to get the party on foot towards the small mountainy lake at which we hoped to ambush the geese. It was late. We could not be there by twilight. We had a mile or more to walk, skipping from tussock to tussock over the chocolate bog.

They stowed me away at last in a neat round hole in the turf, which had the shape of a large keg or small barrel. No wonder it was shaped so, for it had been dug to house a barrel.

In the old days, when poithín was illegally brewed in Eire, the makers had to conceal their kegs of the true, smoky, water-coloured, dangerous, vintage whisky — which was best taken either hot from the still or else, so rarely possible, after being matured. In between these dates, it was a lethal drink, which made people drunk for the second time if they took a glass of water for their thirst next morning. There was a slight blueness in its colour, like the faintest wood smoke. The best way to hide the kegs from the excisemen and the guards was to dig a hole in some hundreds of square miles of bog, and to bury them. I was squatting in such a hole. It was next to the tarn at which we expected the geese, and it made an excellent ambush. My comrades went to other places of concealment.

Incidentally, there was a good economic reason for illicit brewing in distant parts like these. If you had a patch of corn fifteen miles from the nearest market, across bad tracks, and had to carry your harvest there on your shoulders, it was convenient to reduce its bulk. Brewed down at home, it could be carried in one keg on one journey as spirits: in sacks as grain, it might take four journeys.

The geese did come. In fact, they had come already. But it was pitch dark now, without a trace of moon. We could hear their wings, their gabbling on the little pocket-handkerchief of water, but we could not see an inch of them. I was furious with our party of three, including myself, for being a quarter of an hour too late. We could have poniarded those geese by touch, but we could not pistol them. They were invisible.

Like a mad terrapin in a mud-puddle, I glared into the frozen darkness in all directions, my implements clattering about me. And, by, it was cold! In the midwinter poithín-hole, with my shooting mittens and various dodges, I was protected from the icy air a little: but what of Jack and what of that foodless warrior who had no hole to protect them? The boy had such a thin suit over his bird bones, his best one. He was a Spartan with long fingers under his arm-pits, at whose slim breast the fox of January gnawed unprotested.

Eventually they came to fetch me.

The Journey Home

Jack said with chattering teeth: 'Come along now, we can go. It is too late. Nothing can be done now.'

They extended gelid hands to help me out of the keg, while I unbent my bone-blue joints, like the round knobs which butchers hack with hatchets, and muttered about the geese. The setter Brownie, who had been trembling in it with me, was released to scamper.

'We must come again. We must come before sunset, properly. Did you hear them?'

'Yes, yes.'

We blew out our words, beating our arms for circulation.

It will be important to tell this story with clinical accuracy. It is not a fairy-story, and not fiction.

Evidently Jack and his bashful prince of the Gaels must have noticed the things as they came to collect me. But the first of them had heard of it and the second had seen it often before, so they must have decided to find out what effect it would have on the Saxon.

As we tottered the first uneven paces from that agonizing hidey-hole, Jack said, with exaggerated concern and a touch of mischief: 'Look, what is this? Look at this!' He pointed, half teasing, half scared himself, to our feet. And there, at our very boots, a crumbling series of phosphorescent green worms —about as bright as the end of a cigarette — but green instead of red — were tumbling back into the soggy footprints. They were a miniature landslide of light, like a football crowd of crumb-sized spectators pouring out of the exits, all on fire.

It is alarming, whatever you may say, to find that your footprints have turned into glow-worms, in the black night, in the
red bog, fifteen miles from anywhere.

I said: 'Well, it might be anything. Come along; let's go
home.'

We were in a country which believed in fairies — not fairies
with gauzy wings sitting on toad-stools, but supernatural beings
largely malevolent. When your individual unconscious is submerged in the subconsciousness of a place and race, it tends to
be influenced by its surroundings.

The nervousness of me, the materialist, grew contagious.
The other two, a prehistoric believer and a more modern half-
believer, now caught the scare. What had started as one of
Jack's jokes turned into a subdued, silent panic. We began to
hop and shamble away, from tussock to tussock, in the direction
of the darkling settlement where human beings lived.

But, after a hundred yards or so, shame and the scientific
attitude triumphed.

They were ahead, more nimble and more accustomed to the
moorland. I called to them: 'Jack, wait for me. Stop a minute.
Don't leave me alone. I must find out about it.'

They stopped to wait, and we turned.

For a hundred yards back, exactly like the black footsteps of
good King Wenceslas in the white snow, there were three
chains of glow-worm footsteps in the sable night. We looked
from side to side, and now there circled or arc'd us at a distance
a cantering, high-stepping circumference of green fire. It was

made by the feet of my beautiful setter bitch, and it moved
with her.

'No, wait. Don't go away. We must find out.'

I lifted my boot: it was on fire.

I put my finger to the welt of it and scooped a piece: it stuck
to the finger, without burning it.

I smelt it: it did not smell, except of bog.

I gingerly licked it: it tasted of wet turf, nothing else.

It was tasteless, scentless, soundless, warmthless, visible.

We stumbled off through the oceanic night, leaving these
same footprints behind us, circled by the flaming setter,
gradually going quicker and quicker. We joked at ourselves,
partly clowning our uneasiness, but feeling inside a real wish to
get out of here, out of the whelming winter darkness and the
pursuing fire. We took to the bed of a burn, where the going
was better than on the hummocky heather. We were in a hurry
We slid and tripped and fell.

Towards the relief-giving end of this eerie treck, whose
direction in the ink of evening depended on our guide, I did
manage to pass a few messages through Jack to the grandee.

'Do you often get this?'

'Yes.'

'Is it the Will-o'-the-Wisp?'

'No. That one is a different thing. Often we see him too, but
he is more like a tower of flame.'

'What do you call it?'

'We call it the *solas sidh* (the Fairy Fire).'

And the guache, courtly, resentful caballero looked distantly, with dignity into the darkness. He was afraid that I was going to make a mock of him.

We went to the car, not to the dwellings. It was parked at the foot of the track which led to them. We wanted to go away.

No tip was given to our proud conductor. Perhaps, when sufficient time had passed to make it decent, he could be entertained on his next visit to market, with drink or smokes.

We switched on the inside light of the car, like royalty going to the theatre, but for us it was to banish the night. We wanted a bright, small, cosy interior — a shell of civilization to defend us against prehistory, against the principalities of races long defeated. Ireland is a melting pot of conquered cultures, of stone men and bronze men and iron men, of Celts and Vikings and Anglo-Normans, driven remorselessly westward by the volcano of European history, pressed finally together against the rim of the Atlantic in their promontory forts, between the devil of the New Weapon and the deep sea. Their gods go with them. Duk-Duk dancers and Druids, Fir Bolg and Tuatha De Danann, Baal and Beltaine, Crom Cruach and Cromwell, the conquered conquerors, enslaved, revengeful, charged with ancient powers — they pressed heavily in the wind against the weak, lit windows of our motor, tight shut.

We took some whisky from the flask, and drove home thoughtfully, in silence at first.

There seems to be a theory that the *solas sidh* is some kind of phosphorescence — like the lights in tropical oceans — and that it depends on atmospheric conditions. It is not caused by methane or marsh-gas — which may account for the other 'tower of flame' which the boy mentioned — since it does not burn or smell. It is no good going to the Cow Bog in the hope of viewing it, because it only comes when the conditions have happened to suit each other.

Then it is there, glowing like a forgotten kipper in the darkened pantry, but much more so — stepping with the way-farer, step for step — galloping with his dog in cusps and curlicues of ice-green fire — not shewing itself dispersedly, but only on the foot or where the foot has been — cold, corpse-lit, and brighter than the figures on wrist-watches which have been painted with luminous paint.

On other nights, which are the usual ones, no frightful fiend doth tread so closely behind the wildfowler.

LETTER FROM A GOOSE SHOOTER

I FELT lonely standing on the white sand in the twilight. The rowers in the currach cried a farewell to me as they left. Then, in the quickly falling darkness, shot with the goose cries, I went into the broken house on man's first duty — to make fire. When this was burning with wreckage, I set out to search for the well. But it was dark now, and the electric torch had broken somehow, so I could not find it. I went to the drinking place for cattle and got water there.

76

I was alone on the island, and it was mid-winter.

The Inniskeas are islands off the west coast, once inhabited by men. But ten were drowned in 1927, in what was called the Inniskea Disaster, and — the land being too exhausted by a thousand years of 'sea-manure' (sea-weed) to grow potatoes any longer — they had been abandoned. The little village stood quite silent beside its anchorage, the roofs fallen, the stones of the walls in the street. In twelve years it seemed to have lost all human origin. No people were expected by its broken doors. A few black bullocks sheltered there at night, the seals came into the harbour, two small black birds visited it in the mornings, two ravens cronked higher up, and all the time you heard the eternal geese, which, driven away during man's thousand years of residence, had now returned.

The people in the currach had been afraid to leave me, because it was a bad coast. There was a chance that they might not be able to come back in six weeks, as sometimes happened on the next-door neighbour, the Black Rock Light. Also they feared the dead of the disaster and perhaps a certain old god of the island, venerated until the last generation, of whom I was to hear more.

Brownie, the red setter, kept me awake for all but two hours, the first night, shivering. Such bed as we could make was strange. The feelings and thoughts have gone with people about me. But if I had had paper, and could have written, it would have been a fountain of feeling about eternal things. I did write on an envelope, during the strange and sleepless night, a message

of propitiation to the god. The romancing mainlanders had told
me about him already, and I had seen some Inniskea stones in
the Dublin Museum, and I believed what I had been told.

On Inniskea, long before Patrick came,
Stood the stone idol of the secret name:
The magic people made him. No surprise,
No threat, no question lit his two round eyes,
Nor had he other features. Consciousness
Was all his feeling, all his creed 'I wis.'
He watched the wild geese twenty centuries.

Inniskea is an island. Ten years gone
The human race lived here, the windows shone
With candles over the water, and men
Fished currachs, women wellwards went from ben.
There was a King to rule the island then,
Chosen for might, who had his admiral
Of all the Inniskeas. The priest's sick call
Was this cold pasture's only festival.

Mass was so far off, with such storms between,
And in the dark nights moved so much unseen
On the wild waters, that Man's beating heart
Still sometimes turned towards the old God's art.
Much magic was made with the dew. The wells
Secretly stirred with strange internal spells.

78

LETTER FROM A GOOSE SHOOTER

To keep the Agent off, or the Excise,
Fires were lit before the God of Eyes
And dances made around his stone, sunwise.
Their old cold Godstone they, for comfort, dressed
In one new suit each year: his Sunday best.

Then the remorseless sea, the all-beleaguring,
The crafty, long-combed sea, the stark and whistling,
The savage, ancient sea, master at waiting,
Struck once.

Two hours later the mainland
Received one man, a saucepan in his hand,
Astride an upturned currach. At the Inn
They gave him clothes without, whisky within,
Such as they could: but he nor left nor right
Altered his eyes. Only, with all his might,
This man bailed with his saucepan all that night.
In half one hour of squall, from calm to calm, the Main
Holding his ten mates drowned had fallen on sleep again.

Nobody painted the houses after.
The islanders lost all heart for laughter.
Work was a weariness, dances were done,
On the island whose pride of Man was gone.

LETTER FROM A GOOSE SHOOTER

Now I am all alone on Inniskea,
All alone with the wind and with the sea.
The corrugated iron, rusted brown,
Gives a burnt look to the abandoned town.
The roofs are ruins and the walls are down.

The Land Commission took the people ashore.
King Phillip Lavell is here no more.
They have even taken away the God Who Saw,
To stand in Dublin Museum. From ten till four
He eyes the opposite wall.

              Oh God of Eyes,
Bound there in darkness and deprived of skies,
Know that your Geese are back. Know that their cries
Lag on the loud wind as, by candlelight,
At Inniskea's one fire, I, your last subject, write:
Lulled by their laughter, cradled in their night.

It was something I can't explain now, to write this by th
popping of the salty firelight, in the one-roomed house, alone
The crayfish pots were piled high in the corner, with spherica
lobster pots on top of them, twisted out of heather roots. A
bed of hay stood in another corner with damp quilts on it. Th
room was crammed with wreckage (there was a goodish roof t
keep it dry). There were two wooden stools, some seine nets
a bag of flour hanging in the window for castaways, a billy-can
a candle stuck in a bottle, the trembling dog. And outside

Deserted village on Inniskea

F

within twenty yards, there was the lonely sea, the goose music, the heathen god, the winter night of stormy solitude.

The flames of the fire in this primeval cave shone on a brown ceiling of boards.

Three mildewed religious pictures, without frames or glass, hung from a piece of timber beside the bed of straw. They were as necessary to the place, when two or three of the islanders slept there, waiting for wreckage, as lifeboats are necessary to a liner. But to a soul alone, possibly to stay six weeks if the weather broke, beleagured by cold and ghosts and darkness and the sea of night, they were the lifebelt itself. One was of the Sacred Heart, in the middle of a cross. One was of some choristers singing with unnaturally goody-goody faces. And one, in colour, was of Joseph holding lilies and the Infant Christ. His beard was cut like mine. Brownie, a pagan, could find no comfort in these, and that was why she trembled. I stoked the fire and laid her before it, stretching my body across her to give by contact such Christian safety as I could. We slept, in three plaids, on the stone floor, two hours — waking at intervals to keep the fire bright.

At half past five it was too much trouble to pretend sleeping. I brewed tea in the billy-can, with a tot of fiery west-coast rum, and ate slices of bread and butter. The tea, boiled together with sugar, was fine. Then, a little after six, we opened the windy door and stepped into the night.

This door had opened itself once in the middle of the night, and once the candle and fire had simultaneously burned low for a moment, and the spirits, whistling like otters, had swung round the deserted homes.

Now, stepping out, I found myself face to face with the Devil.

He was black, motionless, a darkness silhouetted against the darkness, considering me with ears and horns. I stopped also, and considered him. The horns took shape against the night.

When the door had opened itself, I had stood for two heart-beats, then firmly shut it. When the lights had dimmed, I had sat for two heart-beats, waiting for them to burn again. To the cries of otters I had turned a defiant ear. Now, face to face with Satan, I stood as quietly as himself, for many heart-beats.

We watched each other with curiosity, in the calm of aidless spirits. You can only be afraid when you are clothed with civilization, when you have liens of succour. You can only be frightened when you have a chance of escape. Now that I had no human ties, no roof over my head, no means of escape, I had no fears. The Devil, with the same dignity as I felt myself, moved off quietly in the shape of one of the few black bullocks which were left all winter on the island. I had not frightened him — he did not gallop away with the sudden panic of half-wild cattle — and he had not frightened me.

I stepped on slowly over the fallen stones of the village walls, stones which man could hardly detect except by touch and by the wild sense of animals. The thing was to walk with the patience of prehistory, moving with a balanced body between shapes, at half a mile an hour, knowing only the stones, the fallen roofs, the choked drains, the wreckage, the rocks, and the feeling pace of night.

I was half-way to the place which I had chosen, imagining landmarks which themselves consisted only of the dark, when a thing flew up from under our feet. It circled two or three times invisible, braying like a donkey. The strange cry of the ass does have some quality of levitation about it, and perhaps the ruined walls may have reflected the noise in various directions. There were donkeys on the island, too — but my heart knew it was not these. With the beads in my pocket and the magnum in my hand, I did not fear it. It was possibly a shearwater.

By seven o'clock we were at the fallen gable, and, almost simultaneously, almost directly overhead, there was the first low quack of the geese. I could not see them.

The sun, when he was eventually resounding on Achill and Duvillaun and Innisglora and the distant kingdom of Erris, found us collecting six dead Barnacles and chasing two runners. We were sated with what then seemed a glorious victory, the first time we had killed so many at one flight. Fixed in the memory, now, is the first meteor of a darker darkness, streaking down out of the superb squadron — the soul-satisfying Thump with which he bounced upon the salty land. Then, as the light grew, there had been the crouching under the wall, the white breasts advancing with their thrilling cries and ordered ranks, Brownie ruthlessly held down in cover, the body straightening and the two bangs, the second almost coinciding with the thump of the first goose. This was the first time, out of some three hundred sunrises or sunsets, that I had had what I could truly call a left-and-right at geese. Those two White-Fronts on Carrowmore the previous week, for instance: I had been between them and the wind, had had time to reload, and had killed two geese out of four shots. But today, for the first time in my life, it was Bang-Thump, Bang-Thump — the real McCoy. Twenty years later, I can add with pleasure that it was also my last left-and-right.

The Barnacle Goose was a species I had not handled before. She was earlier in her flight than the grey ones. She had a lower, more monotonous, taciturn, disyllabic, quacking note. She had great vitality from the killing point of view, was as cunning as the grey goose, but did not raise herself in the air when shot at with the same rapid climb as her cousins. This heaviness in soaring was one of her chief differences. In appearance she reminded me of the sixty-year-old spinster aunts who used to frequent England in my childhood. She had the same black shiny gloves, the jet beads, the dress of black and dove-grey garnished with white, the high collar which was introduced by the wife of Edward VII, and she probably kept her toque on with a long black hat pin. The average weight of eight birds — I gave one away and did not weigh it — was four and a half pounds. You thought of her as female, but of all the other geese as male. In the hand she was female. In the air, like all these grand creatures, at whom I could not bear to shoot nowadays, she was a male.

Sleepy and satisfied with murder, we plodded the clean sand back to our burrow, and made more tea and bread and butter. The interior of the little house was a surprise in daylight, for, as the bullocks were liable to break glass windows, the owners of this, the soundest building on the isle, had covered the windows with corrugated iron. It was dark inside, both day and night, a sort of cave-life refuge among the straw and looming lobster pots and smoke.

The forenoon passed pleasantly in a long but profitless stalk of a large party on the other side of the hill. I was filled with happiness, watching them for half an hour. With a good appetite from this, we came back to dinner, which was to be a cold roast chicken we had brought. I had a bite from the breast and plenty of bread and tea, but Brownie had the two legs, the two wings and the carcase. I could not persuade her to eat bread and butter. So, as she had had an unhappy night, I let her have the meat we owned. Chicken bones are not so bad for dogs as people say.

Eating the good bread by the quayside, I heard geese taking a trip, and ducked into a broken door. Peering out with one eye, I saw the main party turn back. But one, evidently a raw recruit, came on over my head. I was half ashamed at killing so many in the morning, and, thinking that there was modera-tion in all things, particularly in regard to Edwardian spinsters, I had decided to slay no more. But this was too much of a temptation. I stood up, pointed the gun at him with a second's hesitation, saw every feather of his breast in the frosted winter sunlight, and the white-scarfed head turning hither and thither as he looked about to discover why he was alone. Then the temptation was too great, and, taking my finger from the choke trigger to the cylinder (where I knew there was a small cartridge of No. 2 shot) I let him have it with the proper lead. Smack! He struggled madly in the air, with one wing broken at the elbow, turned four or five somersaults, and landed thumping on the white sand of the harbour — where Brownie was waiting to receive him. She brought him to me, his live snake head curling upright on one side of her mouth, and, hating the business of screwing the tough neck, I thumped his head on the door post to break his brains.

These geese had been sent over by two men in a currach, who, in fishing the bay, had made a visit to the North Island to brew tea. Now, when I wanted to snatch an hour's sleep, the two rowers of the currach arrived to pay a visit. They were Irish-speakers. They apologized for having the English badly. They danced round me like pleased dogs, delighted by the strange beard-man who had dared the ghosts, giving loud joyful cries of hospitality to their old kingdom, where they had been born in the last century. They had been born on the flat North Island, however, and disapproved my choice of the featured south.

We had high pleasure with each other. I bid them welcome to the south with a glass of rum. They watched me finish my dinner, sitting interested in the dark den, watching my eating manners. We made long talk. The elder of the two always addressed me affectionately, laying his hand upon my sleeve, as 'my *good* man'.

I was told about the Godstone, his yearly suit of new clothes — I gathered they were of blue serge — and how the South Island, once growing jealous of the North's holy possession, stole him away to the South in a currach on a dark night. At about this time a barrel of paraffin was washed ashore, and the King of the South had it brought into the house where the Godstone stood, hidden away behind a curtain at the hinder end. They were experimenting with the paraffin — a novelty to them — in the hope that it would be something to drink, when a child let fire to it, and the house was consumed. One man was burned to death in the flames. But the fire halted at the curtain of the Godstone, and he was untouched. 'You may say what you like, my *good* man, but there was something strange about that, wasn't there?'

I expressed my indignation at his having been taken in chains to Dublin, and asked what he was like. 'We do not know,' said the elder man (Reilly). 'He was in my father's time. A priest,' he added indignantly, 'then came and broke him. But the Godstone hurted his foot, and he was dead within the twelve-month.' 'Do you mean that it fell on the priest's foot?' 'No, no,' cried Reilly testily: 'it hurted his foot.' I was left with a confused guess that there might have been a verse of Scripture, distorted by translation from Irish into English, at the back of his strong mind. He probably had no idea about its being in the Bible: 'Thou shalt bruise his head, but he shall bruise thy heel.'

'Where,' I asked, 'was the Godstone kept when they stole him?' 'Why, in the house you are in now, my *good* man; did you not hear anything last night?'

In the course of great compliments upon staying alone with the spirits, the younger man said strongly: 'If they were to offer me three million pounds, I would not stay alone on the islands. If I had travelled the world a bit' (here he bowed courteously to me) 'perhaps I would stay. But in my present state I would not stay a night alone, no, not for three million pounds.' He giggled at the thought of anybody offering him this sum.

We discussed the thing which brayed, from under my feet. The whistling, they thought, was otters or seals. I whistled in imitation, and the old man, cocking his head on one side, said 'Otters' emphatically. But the braying stumped them. Donkeys could not fly over your head, geese did not bray, and the Godstone would have been too heavy to fly. Anyway, he was supposed to be in Dublin, though I doubted whether he spent the nights there.

Were there any other stones on the island? Yes, plenty. There was a very good one quite close to here, which they would show me when they were showing the well after I had finished dinner. It had photygraphs on it.

The photygraph stone was a thin slab of limestone stuck upright above the harbour. It had a circular cross, like a consecration cross, upon it, and underneath, beautifully carved, the kind of wriggle which you find in the Book of Kells.

There followed conversation about the North Island, dear to

A crucifixion slab on the North Island

them, as yet unvisited by me. They eagerly urged me to come across to it in their currach, but I would not go. A currach is a primeval water vehicle with no keel, kept upright in the sea by faith. It is said to be safe. But I did not care for it, after coming in one of them on this long-rolling sea the day before, and I thought the motor-boat might arrive to take me home while I was away, and at any rate I had taken a dislike for the North Island. It seemed too flat to be interesting. Trying to provoke my interest they pointed out one high, symmetrical, lonely sandhill — the landmark of the island. What did I think it was made of? It was not a sandhill at all. It was made of three things, with the sand piled round them: the three things were stones, shells and bones. 'Bones of what?' I asked, thinking of some prehistoric kitchen midden. 'Men's bones, of course.' 'Good gracious, what sort of men?' 'Oh, it would be those Danes, I suppose,' said the elder Reilly off-handedly. 'A lady came here in the summer,' he added, 'from Dublin. She was digging them up, you know.' Considering the matter, he reported with awe: 'She put a wire fence all round them.'

We had other interesting talk, about the two public houses there had once been (one was a shebeen), and about the dragging home of brides — how only the younger people could go to Mass, and then only on fine days, because it was not safe to take the old people in boats for fear of storm — about the last King of the Island, a big man with a voice like thunder, who was killed by drinking crude rum washed ashore, who spent a month in the Belmullet hospital, but was brought back to his island to die — about a man who had hanged himself from a rafter — about Columkille's church on the North Island — about the whaling station which the Norwegians once made here, and the great Iron they had left.

Then, seeking a little information for themselves, the old man mentioned that the Germans were very thorough men. I agreed. Was I an Englishman, he asked, with hesitation. 'My mother was certainly an Englishwoman,' I said, 'and I was educated in England.' 'Well, that's the way it goes,' said he, rubbing his hands together with delight. A man who could bring himself to live alone with the spirits of Inniskea was to Reilly worth considering.

We arranged to come out to the North Island in a three-man currach in January, there to spend some weeks together in amity. They promised to give me the Gaelic properly ('Fuil Gaedhilge agat?' they had inquired, and I, with stammering tongue and shame, had wrongly made up an answer, 'Ní tá agam'). I was to give them change of thought I suppose. Then, waving their caps gaily in farewell, they pulled out of the harbour, and the currach dwindled over the sea.

The barnacles made no evening flight that sunset. They were upset by the moon, now growing. I guessed that on moonless nights they spent the day on the South Island, the night on the lake of the North, but that when the moon was strong they would fly at whim. I had caught the flight in the morning partly because it was the first quarter of a growing moon — they were not yet taking it for granted — and partly because the clouds had killed the light. Or did the sea-geese have no regular hours?

In our dark home I carefully dried two of the fishermen's quilts before a big fire, hard-boiled four eggs, of which I chopped up two for Brownie (who thought me no cook), drank tea, and made a bed with loving thought. Then I put the beads over my head, to wear them as a talisman which would not need holding, and slept in their protection, half believing. After an hour's deep unconsciousness I woke at eight o'clock, in an agony of cramp. Disposed again in better position — the priest's position for sleep, called 'in Grace' — we sank into the deep world again till midnight: then woke with the roar of the wind outside, and its whistle under the door.

I revived the fire in the now freezing room, and lay listening. They had not wanted to leave us on the island, and I had been forced, pointing to the sack which bulged mostly with the rugs and two saucepans, to say that I had food for a fortnight. But there were only four loaves of bread, two pounds of butter, and a little sugar and tea, with twelve eggs and a pot of Bovril. Brownie was too pampered for these things. I was not troubled about starving, but the dog would lose condition, and a long stay might be a bore. There were enough geese to live on for the rest of the winter. Considering how I would fix up a wooden spit to roast the birds, and how I could eat a green plant from one of the streams, which looked a little like watercress, I fell into a blissful sleep for the third time, till I had slept eleven hours.

I had no geese the third day. The moon had put them off. With so many dead, it did not seem right to stalk them. Going out to the morning flight, I found the wind had dropped. In the afternoon the motor-boat called for us, on her way from relieving the lighthouse at Black Rock. By the evening I was back in a hot bath at our village of five hundred souls on the mainland, feeling as if I was in London, but feeling also a sense of loss in Bedlam. The equanimity and reality which I had collected on the last day, exploring the caverns and strong promontories of the west coast of the island — all the deep racial thoughts I had felt there and a temporary conviction of the relation of God to man — the cairn I had made for the bodies of two of my shot geese, which had been found by the herring gulls before I found them — all the hours on high places, with only a pair of ravens above me: all my strength was momently crumbling away. I can only remember that the North Island was said to be inhabited by one cat, and that, on the last morning, when I was standing by the glorious, lonely Atlantic harbour, wondering whatever other Christmas-present God could think of for me, I had looked up to find a pair of young ravens playing a few feet above my head. They were quite small, only about the size of jackdaws, and every feather on their bodies was perfect. I watched in rapture, admiring the strong re-curve of their glossy primaries and the way they wagged their feather-perfect tails. I thought how strange that young ravens should be as small as jackdaws, that they should have this thin and almost curlew beak. I looked earnestly upon the beak, and upon the feet. My heart bounded as I distinguished the redness, even against the sky. No wonder they were so trim, so much lovelier than any of the black-guard I had previously known. They were not ravens at all. They were the red-beaked choughs of legend, looking on Man for the first time — as I on them.

E went to the island again, in a three-man currach. We got there and back between the weathers. A heron wove her way to the deserted haven as we left it, low and labouring over the slaty sea.

The Godstone had begun to fascinate me. It had become a wild goose chase of its own.

95

I had started a confused, archaeological quest for it — which was unwelcome to the inhabitants of Erris.

They did not want to be investigated as idolators by an infidel. It had happened before, in the case of some interfering Protestant missionaries from Achill, and the search had resulted in calamity. They were partly ashamed of the stone and partly anxious to defend it. My heavy mind — too blunt, direct and Saxon — was bejingled with ideas about paganism and phallic pillars and the claptrap of a half-baked archaeologist. Their reaction therefore, unless carefully stalked, was to maintain that the image never had been worshipped, and was in fact an ordinary Catholic statue before which Creeds, Our Fathers and Hail Marys might be recited. In this, they were not being quite frank.

The thing was called in English the Godstone. In Gaelic, so far as I could catch it by ear, it was called the Naomhóg — that not very secret name, mentioned in the verses which I had written on the island before starting the quest in earnest. Now 'naomhóg' could mean a canoe or a cot. But 'naomh' meant 'saint or holy one' and 'óg' was the adjective for 'young'. The Little Holy One. Incidentally, the word — which looks as if it would sound horrid in English script — looked and sounded beautiful in Gaelic: naoṁóᵹ. They pronounced it 'nee-vogue'. Scrabbling about in a dictionary, I found that 'neamh' meant 'heaven' and 'néam' 'brightness'; but also that 'neamh' was a negative prefix, so that 'neamh-óg', unless I had gone astray in the grammar, might mean the reverse of young: the Old One.

In any case, pursuing the word by ear at first, and not knowing how to spell it, made dictionaries unhelpful.

I chased that Naomhóg for five months all together — a tortuous, Irish trail which is now too complicated to straighten out. The only way to tell it would be as it went.

It was said in one of the country legends that St Patrick failed to bless Erris when he blessed all Ireland from the top of the Reek. It was a low peninsula, mainly of sand-dunes and marram grass, about ten miles long, which formed the outer arm of Blacksod Bay. Its dreadfully poor inhabitants lived mainly by fishing — though there was a small doll-factory — and their gardens were of sand. By digging these gardens with alternate layers of sand and sea-weed, they were able to grow potatoes. They mostly spoke Gaelic. They had abandoned the two narrow, rocky islands of Inniskea, which covered a stretch of about four miles, three miles out to sea, because of the 'disaster' in 1927 and because life on them was said to be 'slavery'. All commodities, including religion and fuel, had had to be imported by boat, for there was no priest. Two other islands, Innisglora and Duvillaun (the Black Island), were also deserted. All had been inhabited by 'saints' — that is to say, by monks — in the seventh century, and long before that by other races, stretching back to people perhaps like Esquimaux, who lived on shellfish. Vikings had raided their waters, as the French lobster-fishermen still did. The islands bristled with prehistory with shell-mounds and beehive huts and stone circles and the

G 97

graves of saints. Within living memory they had had their own admirals and kings. It was by no means improbable that they should have had their demi-gods, particularly since the nearest priest was over the sea. If a man died on the islands, he was left untouched where he lay, even in the turf ashes — for many days if the weather kept the priest from coming — because to touch him before the Church did so was dangerous.

It will madden the Irish Nationalist, and perhaps the fanatical Catholic also, to be told that the people of the islands were primitive. However, they were. They lived in the primitive conditions of nature and were moulded by their surroundings. Nor, I might suggest, did they need to be ashamed of this. If they were barbarous, it was a barbarism less lethal than ours, and if they did reverence a Godstone, at least they gave it reverence. Being primitive need not mean being worse — nor better, for that matter.

Rowing back from our second visit, we held converse with the boatmen of the currach.

I asked Pat Reilly of Glosh why the oars of a currach had no blades. When we had succeeded in explaining what a blade was, he replied — not what an Englishman might have said, 'Oh, we have tried all those, but they are no good: we find these more convenient' — but: 'Well, we have never seen one.'

He told us, as he tugged at the rough pole, that May was the worst month for basking sharks. They did not attack currachs unless struck with an oar, but sometimes they would follow them. The way to 'banish' sharks, when they did so, was to pour in front of them some of the fishy bilge from the boat. This caused them to sink at once.

Disposed to conversation by these more general topics, it was possible to coax him round to the naomhóg.

He said that it was able to stimulate the growth of potatoes. This was why the South Island had stolen it from the North, which had the better soil. His statement sent me off at once on the trail of a fertility god, and some of the questions which I was to ask later were based on it. He repeated most of what had been put in my verses — verses which, I was beginning to see, were inaccurate as to facts, but could not be altered because of rhyme. He advised us to question his uncle at Belmullet.

Another rower mentioned that the priest who threw the God-stone into the sea was called Father O'Reilly.

We were also told to seek out an old man called Anthony McGinty.

We slithered over the bottle-green sea, gay and conversible, creaking and knocking at the makeshift rowlocks, sitting carefully because there was no keel to balance us, practically feeling the sliding waters caressing out buttocks — through the eighth of an inch of tarred canvas which separated us from the Atlantic Ocean, on which we rose and fell like puffins.

Pat Reilly's uncle proved to be seventy-five years of age, a native of the North Island. He stated proudly that he himself was practically an idiot, and that he could remember nothing

whatever about the naomhóg. We could get little further out of
him. What we did gather was, (1) the Godstone was destroyed
fifty years ago; (2) it had been stolen and kept by the South
Island before the old man's time, but he confirmed the story of
the fire; (3) it was given three suits of clothes every year; (4) it
was in the likeness of a man; (5) it was sunk by the priest in the
home harbour — Portavally on Ordnance Survey, i.e. Abhaile,
the Village Haven.

The uncle did not seem reliable. He had a tendency to talk
about shooting, about St Patrick (the shamrock kind) and on
any other subjects which he thought would be suitable for an
English Gintleman. Probably he did not want to tell me about
the stone. It was generally the better-educated witnesses who
felt ashamed of the Godstone, vehemently asserting that it was
an ordinary Catholic statue never 'worshipped', and these
suspected me of trying to prove that Roman Catholics were
idolaters — which I am not trying to prove.

It turned out that there was no such person as Anthony
McGinty.

After a long drive round the peninsula, we finally ran to earth
an eighty-year-old gentleman called Owen McGinty — who did
not correspond to Anthony's description in any particular. He
was not able to speak English. Luckily the huge, good-natured
Land Commissioner, Séan Glynn, who could speak Irish
perfectly, had come with us.

The grubby, hardy, snot-nosed children crowded round the

long car agape, while ancient Owen, invited into it and regaled with a dram or two from a flask whose neck he courteously wiped before returning it, looked straight in front of him into the past, with dimming, oyster-coloured eyes.

His account was fuller and clearer than the uncle's, perhaps because he could give it in his own language, through Séan's translation and tact.

The naomhóg, he said, was a small stone, weighing two or three pounds. It was about as long as your hand. It was shaped like 'an iron' (? smoothing iron). It was of greenish stone. It had originally been 'broken by a pirate'. (An author called Knight, writing in 1834, stated that £20,000 worth of smuggled goods were annually landed on the shores of Erris. But pirates could be anything on the peninsula — could be Vikings or Elizabethan privateers or Spaniards from the Armada or French fishermen or raiders from another island or anybody not understood. History and prehistory and the present existed in these parts on the same plane.) The pirate, who was to us a new character in the story — and we were to hear more of pirates as it unfolded — broke the image very long ago, not within family memories, at the foot of the photgraph stone on the South Island. The photgraph stone, probably a grave-stone cut for himself by one of the anchorites in the seventh century, was called the Grave of Taidhg. The naomhóg was brought originally from Columkille's church on the North Island. Because it had been broken, it had to be kept together with something, and hence the 'suits of clothes'. They were of red flannel. It was stolen by the South Island from the North, but there was no fight about this. On the South Island it was lodged high in the gable of a house — the one I had slept in — in a sort of niche. It was taken out of the house if the weather was required to be fine. It caused potatoes to multiply. There was a prayer which could be said to it in case of sickness. Our informant was actually in the house on the night of the paraffin fire. He confirmed that a man was burnt to death in it, but that the flames halted at the gable of the naomhóg. He was impressed by the fact that the thatch at this end of the roof-tree did not burn. Finally, when McGinty was about ten years of age, a priest called Father O'Reilly cast the Godstone into the sea. He walked out to the rock called Carrigeenduff, in the jargon of the map-makers, and threw it out from there. Ever since then, it had been calm in the sea off this point. Father O'Reilly was dead within the year.

'N.B.,' I thought to myself, 'if we can find out when this priest was buried, whose name has been mentioned twice, we can find out when the naomhóg was committed to the deep.' And I noted also that the virtues of the object were connected with fertility, fire and storm.

Owen McGinty impressed me as being a tired old man, but sharp and not anxious to tell too much. Any miracles? No, none in particular. Any particular person who looked after the naomhóg or was responsible for taking it out? No, anybody could take it out. Any particular day associated with it, any Saint's Day? No.

On the way home, Séan tried vainly to get my mind in tune

with the realities of the West. I was suffering from theories, enthusiasms, exaggerations. Besides, I was a foreigner, and was feeling the situation wrong. I wanted the naomhóg to be a romantic discovery, like the god in my verses. I wanted it to be some pagan idol dragged away from its island to the museum in Dublin — though it was becoming increasingly clear that the stone had not been taken there.[1] I wanted him to be pre-Christian, druidical, limitlessly old and powerful, if possible even priapic. Of course our informants had detected this tendency of mine at once, and reacted in the opposite direction. Séan was trying to put me on a middle course.

It was not that I was quite insensitive. At least I did have the sense to refrain from thrusting phallic theories upon the gentle, simple, chaste and pious primitives who talked to us. I did try to frame questions of this sort with obliquity, and not to be offensive.

I woke in the middle night with an inspiration. The place-names on the map were written phonetically by cartographers who could not speak Gaelic. Duvillaun was Dubh oileán. What was Inniskea? Was it the island of St Kay or Cay or Gedh, as some said, and how was it really spelt? If it was Inis-sgeithe, could it mean the Island of Fear; or, if it was Inis-cé, could it mean the Island World, like Atlantis? And Inis-sgíthe might mean the Island of Rest.

[1] Mlle Henry had taken two grave-stones to Dublin not the Godstone.

With the Island of Rest, I was off at full tilt. Why could it not be Tir-na-n-Óg, the Island of Youth, where the mythological hero Oisín — the Ossian of the eighteenth century — was taken by the golden-haired, immortal beauty whose name was Niamh? Niamh! And the 'óg' in Tir-na-n-Óg! Niamh-óighe! Was it possible, could it be possible, let it be possible, that Inniskea was the veritable Land of Youth which coloured so much of Irish legend, and let my naomhóg be none other than the girl Niamhóighe, Young Neave, who took Oisín on his wanderings! So far as I could remember the wonderful rendering of this legend by W. B. Yeats, she took him to three islands. They went to the Island of Youth, where everybody danced and was eternally young; to the Island of Battle, where he fought the demon of the cave; and to the Island of Sleep or Forgetfulness, where the giants rested.

There were exactly three main island-groups off the coast of Erris! There was Innisglora, where the soil had the property of preserving bodies from decay — and what could correspond better with the legendary island of immortality, the Land of Youth? There was Duvillaun, the Black Island — and surely a black island suited well with the Island of Battle? Finally there was Inniskea, which might mean the Isle of Rest — and what more extraordinary than that there should be a real naomhóg on it, which pronounced itself so much like Naimh-óighe, the conductress of Oisín?

What were Yeat's sources? Presumably they derived through Michael Comyn from the Fenian cycle and the voyage of

Bran. What was the date of the Fenian cycle, what of Bran — for St Brendan really was connected with the neighbour isle of Innisglora — and with what parts of Ireland were they hitched up?

I fell asleep in a rapture of discovery, deciding to get books and books from Dublin and to write to the Irish Folklore Commission. It was a sleep sweetened by the sound of the Bell Branch, among the drowsing, feather-ear'd giants of Yeats, in whose beards and hair the colonies of owls had built their nests, 'filling the fibrous dimness with long generations of eyes'.

Our next contact poured cold water on such fancies.

It had dawned on me that we could not get much farther by questioning the old people ourselves. I was too strange for them, too dangerous, too mixed with the tradition of oppressors, and my car was much too grand. Their natural speech was Gaelic, and even in the gentle translations of Séan they were not at home. Their tender, primitive, suspicious minds were unhappy in forthright cross-examination. They were not suspicious in a mean way. They were like antelopes in the presence of some other animal, possibly carnivorous.

In these circumstances, I had a second inspiration. I would offer a small money prize to the schoolchildren of the peninsula, for the best set of answers to a questionnaire, and another prize, as camouflage, for the best essay in Gaelic on Inniskea. We would advise the children, avid for the great reward and honour of prize-winning, to extract the facts from their grandparents

— who might talk more freely to their own blood, in their own homes and language.

To put this plan into action, I needed the help of the school-mistress.

Miss Cronin was a strong-minded, admirable, not hostile, middle-aged, dedicated, educated but not scholarly woman, of high Catholic principle. She would do anything for the children. She wanted them to have the excitement of the competition. But she was determined not to let me get away with any heretical interpretations, derogatory to the islanders.

This brought up another side of the detective story. Every statement on the subject of the Godstone was liable to be tainted by two or three slants, apart from natural suspicions against myself. The creature had been mentioned once or twice in print, as we were to find later, and these mentions were not unknown to the locals. They might at any moment read the published statements back to me, not giving their own observations, but reproducing the printed word. The second taint was that Miss Cronin herself was liable to impose her strong character and, may I say without unkindness, her prejudices, on the very children who were answering the questionnaire. Finally, the islanders had a delicacy of mind which tended to suppress unwelcome information. They were aware of the schoolmistress's orthodox feelings, and, to her, they were unwilling to dwell on matters of piseóg (sorcery).

Here was Miss Cronin's attitude to the subject.

The naomhóg was not pagan at all. Canon O'Reilly, who took

great interest in it, proved this. No, she was not referring to he Father O'Reilly who threw it into the sea but to a Canon)'Reilly, who came afterwards. He proved that the naomhóg as an Italian terracotta statuette of the Infant Jesus. This was rought to Inniskea long, long ago, nobody knows how. But ome pirates arrived who set fire to all the houses on the island. 'he only one which would not burn was the one which had the nfant Jesus in it. The pirates inquired why the house would ot burn, and the islanders informed them of the reason. So the irates took the statuette out and broke it. But, when they were one, the islanders collected the pieces and fitted them together. t did not look quite so nice, now that it was broken, so they nade a red flannel dress for it. They made a new dress each ear, out of reverence. A strange feature was that whenever hey came to put on the new dress, they would find the old one vorn out, just as if it had been worn by a living man. Then there ame some Protestants, who were very kind to the islanders and ave them food, etc. and the result was that the trustful islanders old them all about their naomhóg, and the Protestants went way, promising to come back in six months with plenty more ood. No sooner had they arrived in Dublin, however, than they vrote to the *Irish Times*, saying that on the island of Inniskea here were people who called themselves Catholics who wor-hipped a pagan idol. Father O'Reilly was at that time the P.P. n the mainland — not the Canon O'Reilly who came after and roved things, but Father O'Reilly, called Big Father Pat)'Reilly, to distinguish him. When he read this article in the

Irish Times he went straight out to the island and destroyed the statuette of the Infant Jesus. All this happened at the time of the Famine. No, it need not necessarily have been the great famine year: there were several famines in Inniskea. Big Father Pat O'Reilly's grave had a tablet in Binghamstown Church, so you could find out the date of his death. After he was dead, Canon O'Reilly came to Belmullet, and took a great interest in the naomhóg. He proved it was a terracotta statue of the Blessed Infant. He asked the islanders to dive for it, at the place where it had been thrown into the sea, and, after great trouble, they managed to bring up the pedestal of the statue. Canon O'Reilly kept this. Miss Cronin did hear that he gave it to the Dublin Museum, but when she went there she could not find it. Canon O'Reilly wrote something about the holy statue. Perhaps you could find out what he wrote from the O'Reillys-at-the-corner-by-the-Post-Office, in Belmullet. She believed they kept or disposed of his books. Yes, she did hear that prayers could be said in front of it, for stormy (to keep off pirates) or fair weather, but they were Christian prayers. No, she did not hear about the fertility of potatoes. No, it had no connection with St Martin. (Miss Cronin knew as well as I did the antecedents of St Martin.) No, she did not hear that Big Father O'Reilly was dead within the year.

Now Miss Cronin was kindly disposed towards me and she was not trying to falsify the evidence — which she had gleaned from the Canon. But her opinions and his opinions and the terracotta bambino which he had piously wished on himself left several questions unanswered. It remained a fact that the English name for the naomhóg, used by the islanders themselves, was Godstone — surely a meaningful name: that it was connected with fertility and weather and fire: and that it had been destroyed by a Catholic priest. I still do not think that I was being tiresome in questioning its nature. I wanted to know how big it was, whether it was worked stone or perhaps a meteorite, whether it was all or part of a statue or grave slab, whether it was connected with spring or autumn, what miracles or virtues resided in it, and why people had thought it important.

Miss Cronin agreed to distribute the questionnaire.

A trip to Dublin confirmed the fact that the image was not there. I also got hold of some books of reference — to which a letter from Séan Ó Suilleabháin of the Folklore Commission had given a clue. Here are the known printed references which seem to bear on the subject.

Caesar Otway, a Protestant cleric, wrote in 1839 (*Tour in Connaught*): 'One of the company mentioned his having visited Inniskea; and that, as usual, the people are beset with gross superstition. They have a wooden idol there, left by a holy priest, who said that as long as it was preserved with reverence, no loss of life by shipwreck would happen to any of the islanders, who always worshipped the idol before venturing to sea. He said that (as he was informed) this idol was once stolen by smugglers, who supposed that they carried their palladium while they kept this wooden saint on board; but from the day they stole it until it was returned, which, with all repenting speed, they hastened to do, they were persecuted by a revenue cruiser, and vexed by storms, and driven up and down on the ocean; for how could they have luck when they had no grace, and stole from the Inniskeans their teraphim, their little god.'

The author of *Sketches in Erris and Tyrawley* (1841) said: 'The information I have been able to collect from Mr Crampton and others, concerning Inniskea is limited (Mr Crampton not having had any opportunity, more than I did, of landing there). There are two ancient sepulchral mounds on it, and it contains a few inhabitants, who know nothing of the fated crane, that old writers say is to stand there till the "crack of doom". He *may* be there, but no one in these days ever saw him; but they have what is better, called by some the Neevoge, or, as others pronounce it, Knaveen; both mean "the little saint" and I prefer the latter pronunciation, which may not be a bad derivation from the English word Knave, Latin, gnavus — a knowing fellow. For the knaveen of Inniskea must be a knowing one indeed, for, by his instrumentality, the natives consider they can raise or allay a tempest; raise a storm when a ship nears the island, and so they may get in a wreck; or allay it when their own boats are out at sea in a gale of wind. The knaveen is a stone image of the rudest construction, attired in an undyed flannel dress, which is every New Year's Day renewed. Of course the knaveen has his annals, one event of which may be worth stating:—Some years ago, a pirate happening to land on he island, amused himself by setting fire to the houses of the people, all of which burned but too readily, save one; and the ferocious leader thus seeing one house untouched, urged on with menaces his followers to consummate their destructive doings by burning *this* also; but they could not; as often as they applied fire to it, it went out; they might as well burn one of the ocean rocks. Observing this, he ordered the house to be diligently searched, and finding the "knaveen", he commanded that the holy image should be smashed to pieces with a sledge. Perhaps he was told of the "knaveen's" power not only of arresting fire, but of raising wind, and, as he often roved along the coast, he of course did not desire to leave the storm-compeller in the hands of those to whom he had been so cruel. Thus, having had his wicked will, the pirate sailed away, it is hoped never to return. But the natives, the moment he was gone, collected the fragments of the Saint, bound them together with thongs of skeepskin, and to keep him warm and pleasant, dressed him out in a suit of flannel, which, as we have already stated, is renewed from year to year. It is, however, considered that the "knaveen" has never fully recovered the treatment he received from the pirate's sledge-hammer, nor are they quite so sure of his power over the elements. Perhaps, after all, this is not so much the fault of the idol as of their failing faith. He still, however, is fervently kissed, and had in reverence by all.'

The Godstone was mentioned superficially in *Further Memories of the West* by Sir Charles Robinson, somewhere about the eighteen eighties.

Finally, a Mrs Padden,[1] once a teacher on Inniskea and in 1939 living in Belmullet, aged about 75, kindly wrote this down for me:

'There was a stone in Inniskea shaped like a pillow, and the natives treasured it, as the relic of a saint who lived one time on the island, they said it was the saint's pillow worn in the middle like the shape or mark of a head. Some tourists went in to visit the island, and after they left this place they published in foreign journals that the Islanders of Inniskea were pagans and worshipped idols. The Catholic Church ordered the parish priest to go in and destroy that relic and cast it into the sea. The islanders recovered it and the priests were told of it and they went in again and found the relic or neevogue as it was called dressed in a robe of flannel made from the first fleece of the year. They took the robe off it and burned it in the house of a man named Keane, and broke up the neevogue and cast it into the depth of the sea. The curate died some time after, and the parish priest contracted a cold in his head (coming from the island) as he thought, which turned out to be a serious disease called "Polypus". He had an operation and never recovered consciousness. The man named Keane was called the King of the island, and himself and all his family died except two girls, their mother brought them into the nearest town Belmullet and they also died. The islanders used this Neevogue praying to it that the saint who used it for a pillow, and who was now in heaven would intercede with Almighty God to calm

[1] Mrs Padden is represented by F in the questionnaire later on.

The Main Street, Belmullet

H

the seas to get help and aid in sickness and foodstuffs i
Hunger.'

On Ash Wednesday, while the population of Belmullet walke
the streets with an ash cross drawn on their foreheads, I calle
at Reilly's-next-the-Post-Office after Mass, to ask whether the
possessed any of the supposed papers, mentioned by Mi
Cronin as having been left by Canon O'Reilly-who-came-after
(the priest who invented the terracotta bambino). It seeme
probable that the canon had looked up 'naomhóg' in th
dictionary, found that one of its meanings was 'crib or cradl
and that he had constructed his theory of the Infant Jesus o
this basis.

Mr Reilly-next-the-Post-Office, a courtly, continental sort
gentleman, soon broke me of my English manners. I had gon
breezily into his back-shop, and was already stating my busines
when Mr Reilly, who had risen to welcome me, said politel
'Mr White, I believe?' 'Mr Reilly?' 'The same.' So we bowe
shook hands and began again.

No, Mr Reilly did not think he had any of the papers left b
the canon, but he would make a careful search. Father Lavel
of Pollatomish might quite possibly have some, and I had bett
write to him. The naomhóg was an interesting subject. Big
Father-Pat O'Reilly, who destroyed it, was an uncle of M
Reilly-next-the-P.O. He, the Big Father, died very sudden
shortly after destroying the naomhóg, and the innocent islande
said there was a connection between the two events. W

laughed at this. But did he die actually within the year, I asked, just as the islanders said? Mr Reilly was not prepared to say this for sure, but certainly he died soon after, and unexpectedly. I forgot to ask what of.

In Mr P.O. Reilly's back-shop there were two good maps, of Belmullet as projected and of the Barony of Erris, by Knight in 1834. There was also an excellent reproduction of a peregrine stooping on a mallard, and a stuffed Tawny Owl, mouldering. Mr Reilly escorted me to the front door, and the last I saw of him was his neat bow tie, his keen, pale, Italian face, and the black cross smudged disconcertingly on his courteous forehead.

I went home and wrote to Father Lavelle.

I drove to the graveyard at Binghamstown and found that Big Father Pat had died on the 19th of November, 1876.

By now, the answers to the questionnaire had come in. There were twenty-eight mimeographed questions, which had been answered by six children, after consulting their elders. The elders were: Sorcha bean ní Maoineachan (then aged 76), Brígid ní Maoineachan (60), Sorcha bean ní Maolfabhail (70), Séan Ó Maoineacháin (65), Antoine Ó Maoineacháin (68), Brigíd bean nic Phaidin (73). Call them A, B, C, D, E and F.

1. *What shape was it?* A: A spotted stone, white and brown, an altar stone, like a cross. B: Shape of a human corpse resembling the Blessed Virgin. C: Shape of a nun. D: Like a woman. E: Like a woman, F: A smoothing iron.

2. *How much did it weigh?* A: One and a half pounds. B: No

idea. C: One stone. D: Two stone. E: Two stone. F: Two stone.

3. *How long was it?* A: No idea. B: Two foot, six inches. C: One foot by half a foot. D: Two foot. E: No idea. F: Three foot.

4. *What colour was it?* A: Brown outside and white spots inside. B: Grey-green. C: Grey-green, but red within when broken. D: Grey-green. E: Grey-green. F: Colour grey-green that was in it, but when a little bit was broken off, she was red inside.

5. *Was it any kind of stone?* A: Limestone. B: No idea. C: Limestone. D: Don't know. E: No idea. F: Clay that was in it.[1]

6. *Was it a broken part of a statue?* A: Not an image, but a cross. B: No. C: Not a statue, but a stone with a picture of a Virgin cut on it. D: Entire statue. E: Entire (literally, 'they say that it was all made that was in it'). F: No.

7. *Was it polished or rough?* A: Smooth. B: Polished. C: Polished. D: Polished. E: Smooth. F: Smooth.

8. *Any writing or carving on it?* A: No. B: No carving. There was something written on it. C: Picture of person cut on stone, no writing. D: No writing or carving. E: No writing or carving. F: No writing, but person cut out on the face of the stone.

9. *Was it a meteorite?* A: No. B: No. C: No. D: No. E: No. F: No.

10. *Did it do any miracles?* A: Yes. If the day was bad and the people took it out and said prayers that the storm would abate,

[1] Perhaps a trace of the Canon's terracotta?

when the prayers were said, it would. When the sea-pirates[1] were coming they would start and say the prayers and the sea would rise and the pirates would not be able to come ashore. Some people say that it was Deacon Lyons (Díagan Laiginns)[2] who threw it into the sea at Carraigín Dubh and that he did not live for a year after. 'The sea is always calm at the place where it was thrown out.' B: 'It is the first miracle she made and this is the reason they found out that anything miraculous pertained to her. For there were people coming inside on the island one time, and their name was pirates. They came to the island and they put fire within every roof but they were not able to put a burning on the roof in which the naomhóg was. They searched inside and found the naomhóg in it in a window. They took her and broke her with a stone and they lit the roof. Then they went away. When the people of the island went back to their homes they gathered up the naomhóg and put the three pieces together and a piece of red flannel and they hung her up again. The second miracle. They were starting to distribute a barrel of oil and they put fire to the house and when the fire came to the room where the naomhóg was, the fire went out.' (Then follows third miracle, as related by A.) C: Almost identical with A. D: Identical with A plus B, but 'the pirates threw the naomhóg over the Grave of Taidhg and when the pirate turned round he broke his foot. E: Identical, but stresses that the potatoes

[1] Could these have been Excisemen?
[2] Archdeacon Lyons was a cultured Catholic priest living locally in 1840.

flourished best in whichever island the stone was on — a statement also made by A, B, C, D and F. F: 'It was as follows the way that they found out miracles were with her.' (Otway's story of the pirates is then related, almost in Otway's words.) When they found the naomhóg within the house, in a window a pirate named Seúinín[1] 'threw it over a grave that is on the island of the south in Iniscéidhe[2] that is called the Grave of Taidhg and it broke in three pieces. No sooner was she broken at him than he fell over and made two pieces of his back.' (Then follows the story of the putting together, the thongs, and the flannel which got worn out in the right places every year.)

11. *Did it increase fertility of anything besides potatoes?* A: Not answered. B: Not answered. C: Not answered. D: Only potatoes. E: Only potatoes. F: Potatoes and wheat.

12. *Was any Saint's day connected with it?* A, B, C, D, E and F: No.

13. *Was it taken out in spring or autumn?* A: Only when needed. B: In spring for potatoes. C: Only when needed. D: No. E: In time of storm only. F: In time of need for potatoes or storm.

14. *Any particular ritual or any particular day?* A, B, C, D, E and F: No.

15. *Where was it thrown in the sea?* A, B, C and D: Carraigín Dubh. E: 'Into the ship's pool at Carraigín Dubh.' F: 'From Carraigín Dubh, a couple of yards into the sea.'

[1] Often a contemptuous nickname applied to the Saxon, like Fritz or Jerry to a German.
[2] Note spelling.

The sixteenth question was about the meaning of a name on Ordnance Survey, and turned out to be beside the point.

17. *Where did the naomhóg come from?* A: From the church of Cuilm Cille (North Island). B: They say that a saint made it. C: As A plus B. D: Nobody knows. E: 'They say that it was from the hospice graveyard that the naomhóg first came.' F: 'It is not fixed what place she came from.'

18. *What do you think the word means?* A: 'They say it was a holy woman who was in it long ago.' B: Don't know. C: As A. D: Don't know. E: 'There was the shape of a saint in it, and this was why it was called the naomhóg.' F: Don't know.

19. *What were the words of its prayer?* A, B, C, D, E and F: Seven Our Fathers, Seven Hail Marys, Seven Glorias. E and F added one Creed.

20. *Did any particular person have to look after it?* A, B, C, D, E and F: No. F added: 'There was no caretaker at all, but they always kept her in the same house.'

21. *Who were the pirates who first broke it and whence came they?* A: 'It is said that it was people from the colony of Achill who broke it first and the man who broke it when he turned round he broke his foot and he did not live a year.'[1] B: 'The people of Achill, and they broke her in summer.' C: 'They say that the people of Achill put anger on the priest which caused him to throw it.' D: Don't know. E: 'Sea-pirates broke her at the Grave of Taidhg.' F: Nobody knows.

[1] The colony of Achill was a Protestant colony founded to convert Catholics by a man called Nangle in the early years of the nineteenth century. It still existed.

22. *Why was it dressed in clothes, and what sort of clothes?*
A: After the women had put the pieces together it did not look too good. B: Red flannel. C: After being put together, 'there was not much tidiness in it.' D: Red flannel to hold it together. E: A yard of red flannel to keep it together.

23. *Did it have a different suit at different seasons?* A, B, C, D, E and F agreed that it did not, but had a new one yearly.

The twenty-fourth question resembled the sixteenth.

25. *Was the naomhóg more useful to women than to men?*[1] A, B, C, D, E and F: Either No or No Answer.

The twenty-sixth question resembled the twenty-fourth and sixteenth.

27. *Any connection with St Martin?*[1] A, C and E: No answer. B and D: No. E (who was a firm adherent of orthodoxy): No connection at all.

28. *How would you spell it?* A, C, E and F: No answer. B and D: naoṁóᵹ.

After translating all these and the children's essays — with help, a dictionary and painful toil — I took Miss Cronin's advice and divided the prize between a boy and girl who had collected F and B. We also awarded a bonus of one shilling's worth of sweets to all entrants.

In Miss Cronin's comfortable home, we came to grips once more on the subject of our discoveries up to date. The school teacher, although she was pleased that the prize had gone to an

[1] A tactful question.

orthodox entry, was still my enemy. She was a strong and generous enemy, not mean or bigoted, unusually well-informed, and she surprised me by one courageous admission. Although she had herself sent the Irish Folklore Commission an account of the naomhóg which fitted the Canon's story, she now agreed, after examining the old people's evidence, that the Infant Jesus theory (terracotta) was not tenable any longer. This did not make her relax her hostility to pagan interpretations.

We were now sure that, whatever the nature of the Godstone, it had a verifyable history. Within the past century at any rate, we knew that it had been dressed in red flannel to keep it together, had been sneered at by the Rev. Caesar Otway in 1839 and by Nangle's Protestant colony from Achill, on famine relief, at a later date. The news of Protestant carping had caused a Catholic priest to throw it into the sea from a named rock just before 1876.

But we were in no agreement on the nature of the object.

'The naomhóg *must* have been a statue of a Christian saint,' said Miss Cronin, 'otherwise it could not have performed all these miracles which we know of.'

'But, Miss Cronin ...'

'And in any case, Oisín was a real person. I have seen his grave.'

'Well, all right, even if he was a real person. What I am trying to say ...'

'These fires and storm-quellings were miracles. They happened when the people recited seven Our Fathers, seven

Hail Marys and seven Glorias before the naomhóg. If the naomhóg had merely been a grave-stone from the North Island, or if it had been something out of mythology, God would not have allowed the miracles. Therefore the naomhóg was the statue of a saint. *I feel sure.*'

'Miss Cronin, now listen. It is you who are behaving like a Protestant and me who is talking like a Catholic. The Church has not pronounced the miracles to be authentic: in fact, it has done the very opposite. It was a Catholic priest who threw it in the sea.'

'I *know*,' she said, and the end of this story will show whether she was right or wrong, 'that the naomhóg was an article of Christian veneration. It had *nothing* to do with Niamh or the Land of Youth. The islanders, Mr White, are not like what you think.'

'Even if it was a Christian relic, don't you see that rumours about it, on the mainland, might have given rise to a garbled story about Niamh? Crampton does say that the enchanted land was between Inniskea and Innisglora, and I think I read somewhere that Michael Comyn was no stranger to Connaught. Besides, what about the island being called Inis-sgíthe, the Island of Repose, just like in the Niamh legend?'

'It could just as well be Inis-kéidhe, the island of St Kay. She was a *real* saint.

'And besides,' added Miss Cronin, 'the Island of Repose could be meant in a religious sense, like a Retreat. It could be the island where hermits went to repose.'

'Very well, we had better have another questionnaire, based on the first one. We'll narrow it still further, now that we have got as far as this.'

She said firmly: 'Oh, we won't bother the children any more: I can find out all these things for you myself.'

I could have torn my hair. I did not want any part of what she was likely to find. I wanted the direct evidence of elderly eye-witnesses. I did not know that I had it under my hand already. I was allergic to derivatives from terracotta bambini. Miss Cronin was truthful, sincere, willing to waste her time on me, and generous enough to drop that Canon's Infant Jesus when faced with the evidence. But she was bound, I thought to myself despairingly, bound to colour her findings unconsciously, because of her acute, strong, prejudiced mind. We shall see how far she was prejudiced, in the sequel.

Meanwhile, the pursuit of Canon O'Reilly's supposed papers, left by will, was proceeding through the Post Office. Mr Reilly-next-the-Post-Office, whose nickname turned out to be Tossie, had mentioned Father Lavelle — who, being eventually run to earth, turned me over to Father Durkin — who turned me back to Lavelle — who played me on Father Munnelly — who, presumably thinking that I had better be diverted from the district, revealed the existence of a Mrs O'Donnell of Newport — to whose deceased husband the Canon's Inniskea papers were said to have been left. In order to stop that earth quickly,

I may as well say here and now that Mrs O'Donnell proved to be a dead end.

It was blowing hard, and I was looking at the sky. Mr Tossie Reilly, smiling politely from his shop door, observed that it was 'real naomhóg weather'. I asked about the idiom, and he told me that the last few days of March — I think he said the last two — were called naomhóg days, and wind was expected on them. Why was I interested in the weather?

A road near Belmullet

124

I explained that I had become fascinated by the Inniskeas, and went there whenever I could. I had contracted for a currach next morning, to explore the northern island, and was wondering about the sea.

Mr Reilly advised me to try Padden's motor-boat, and wished me a pleasant excursion.

Padden's second-best motor-boat took a party of us, hastily gathered together, to both the islands. We visited the South Island first. I gave the slip to the others and made off to search for a 'nunnery' marked on Ordnance Survey, and to take photographs.

I wish I could give a picture of those deserted shores, at this distance of time. Going south from the lonely Home Port of the southern island, you soon came upon a landscape of stone. You seemed to be leaping or stumbling or limping or scrambling over a terrain like some sort of Giant's Causeway, under the gentle, ancient, smoothed, poor, featureless, sheep-nibbled swell of the island's one hillock, with its sea-mark and stone walls. Below, the pilgrim was in a chaos of stone. I was back in the lovely solitude of my first visit.

At what the map called Ooghnabraddagh — a chasm in the small cliffs framing an inlet of the Atlantic — I gazed upon the largest seal I had ever seen. He floated abstractedly, sinking for a few seconds every now and then, considering my personality with grand, voluptuous, oafish, idle detachment. Sloth was his deadly sin, if he had one. His head seemed as big as a horse's. The long, round, grey skull, with its non-committal bulging eyes, looked like a gas-mask floating on the sea. We watched each other for ten minutes, without passing any message. I gave him neither fear nor love nor speculation, and he did not succeed in conveying thoughts to me. It was a pure examination, something on a par with pure mathematics. I could have wounded him dreadfully with the gun on my forearm, for we were less that fifty yards apart. Rising and sinking, ruminating with soup-dark eyes in the grey dog-head, I left him to his Blimp-like oceanic siesta.

I had built a goose-cairn to house the bodies of two barnacle geese, shot during that despicable battue on the previous Christmas, but found by herring gulls before I found them. It was still there.

Everything on the Inniskeas was a cairn. Everything was a monument. Westminster Abbey was a babe-in-arms to many things there.

In the ages of prehistory, which were somehow on the same plane as today for most of the natives of Erris, perhaps the barren earth had been a gracious one, cohering with grass. Some sort of ancient people like the inhabitants of Greenland had once accumulated their kitchen-middens here, erected their megoliths — Stonehenge itself, incidentally, was a modern import from the west — and had watched the ages of stone and bronze and iron pass out of date into the Atlantic mist. One of the evacuated islanders once said to me in a matter-of-fact voice, while discussing the evacuation of 1927: 'We have gone, but there will be another Race.'

Later, when the islands had separated from the coast, and the green soil, like some dust-bowl in America, had begun to fall apart, there had come a colony of Christian hermits between the sixth and the tenth centuries — centuries very long before 1066, the date at which Englishmen assume the world to have begun. These hermits, or religious communities of monks, or saints, had lived humbly on top of the middens, still firm enough with grass to hold the foundations of stone beehive-huts in the encroaching sand, until another race of raiding Vikings smashed them up.

The Viking pirates, driven back or assimilated after they had ruined or mated with the Christian community, had produced a new culture of complications, upon which the Norman invasion of Ireland had impinged. Coins had been found here of Henry II and Richard I. For centuries the now 'Irish' inhabitants had slaughtered and raided and betrayed among themselves. Then Englishman had overlaid Norman, and persecutions of religion had overlaid one another, so that a seventeenth-century chalice, pectoral cross and pyx of silver, dated 1669, had been left by some priestly refugee, to be dug up in recent times.

History had grown towards the nineteenth century, from which, backwards, grew my naomhóg, now a historical reality.

But it was all cairns and monuments and mementoes. When a Christian hermit found a pagan pillar, he baptized it with a cut cross. He inoculated it thus with innocence and adopted it to himself. The god Baal turned into Balor or into Beelzebub, a devil. Prometheus the fire-bringer turned into Satan, on fire.

There was practically nothing on the islands which had not been hallowed from some other thing, which was not a memorial to something else — a relic, adapted, a cairn. My goose cairn, though I was not aware of it then, was exactly on top of a monument called Laghta Wirraid in Ordnance Survey — 'Margaret's Stones'. I had adapted the memorial of some saintly Margaret to the memory of two geese.

Imagine all this abandoned. Imagine in the rocky, almost Galapagos landscape, nothing but the wondering Englishman and his setter bitch, and the controversial ghosts of Norman and Saxon and Gael and Scandinavian, and St Brendan (who discovered America and dwelled upon the next door crag of Innisglora) and various Esquimaux with bone pins, perhaps cannibals, gnawing fibulas cracked for marrow, and a seal, and a basking shark, and a whale — there was plenty of whalebones on the islands — and the supernal geese, who were immortal.

Nothing else.

Over the thymey short grass I got back to our shooting picnic, and we chugged away in the motor-boat to the North Island.

Now the force of history hit me in the face.

On this small area of desertion, scarcely a mile and a half long, there were the remains of a promontory fort, a tiny drystone church dedicated to St Columba, three main bailey-mounds of fabulous antiquity, and about five kitchen middens.

Promontory forts were among the most touching and terrible

constructions of Gaelic prehistory. Driven always farther and farther west by the new weapons springing up behind them in the breeding grounds of European strife, the defeated races had thronged or huddled or been hustled to the outer rims of the world — in this case to the Atlantic ocean. And there, literally with their backs to the sea, between the devil and it, they would choose a cliffy promontory jutting into the deep and they would build a gigantic wall of unmortared stones across its base. Behind this wall, their rear defended by the ultimate rollers, they hoped to make a final stand. The sea had demolished most of the one on North Inniskea.

The three main mounds were called the Bailey mór, the Bailey beag and the Bailey dóighte: the big, the little and the burnt settlements. They were sand-dunes now, based perhaps on kitchen middens, or on previous hearths. When the eremitic saints took them over, there had been enough grass to hold the foundations of their single-celled, stone beehives — like igloos. The great bailey was about sixty feet high.

Standing on top of it in the drifting sand, among the etiolated, clean relics of a monastery which had perhaps been founded by a disciple of St Columba, we gazed upon crucifixion slabs like the one shown on page 90, cut thirteen or fourteen centuries ago — upon the skull, rolled carelessly on the golden, salty, aseptic ground, of him who perhaps cut it — on bits of bone and ashes — on the white quartz stones which, except for clay pipes, are all the ornaments still afforded for the dead by western graveyards — on ruined igloos — on Columba's roofless church

I

The Bailey mór

to the westward, hardly five paces long, with its holy-water stoup cut from the living stone, and its fitting lid from the same rock — on the modern village with its skeleton roof-beams, inhabited till 1927, now abandoned like everything else. It was a soul-satisfying abandonment, not a desolate one. The peace and cleanness of desertion had been replenished, had been filled to the brim with calm. It was still the isle of hermits.

The beehives or igloos were perhaps twelve feet in diameter. They had hearths and bed places for short men, enclosed by upright slabs, and stone pillows. The roofs had fallen in.

Looking down ruefully — rueful for this century, not for theirs — on that holy, desiccated, pleasant skull, I began to understand Miss Cronin. I picked up a rib of a sheep or a saint

– it did not seem to matter which — for a keepsake, and, on the way back to the motor-boat, extracted two sharp teeth from the entire skeleton of a basking shark. Then, with teeth and bones, which really symbolized the islet, and with a tranquillity about saints who to me no longer seemed to need to be connected with fertility gods or phallic symbols, we spluttered home, sleepy and hungry, to the real world.

It was time to begin setting things straight.

Suppose that old Mrs Padden, the school-teacher so condescendingly represented as F in the questionnaire, had been right in almost every particular?

Then the naomhóg would have had a history something like this.

A hermit of the sixth or seventh century may have dwelt in one of the igloos, using a stone for a pillow. The answers as to size and weight in the questionnaire had mostly fitted with this, and Mrs Padden had said that it was shaped like a smoothing iron. His head might have worn a depression or shape in this stone, or he might have chosen it because it had such a depression, or it might have had a cross cut on it. The original pirates might have been those very Vikings who came from the north with their long swords of iron, round about the tenth century, to shatter the early Christian monastic settlements of learned Ireland. During the sack of the Island of Retreat, fire had been used. The third of the baileys was still called the burnt one. Perhaps the fire had stopped at the hermit's pillow? Reverence being now attached to his relic, and the Scandinavians settling down with their victims, perhaps it had begun to be venerated for its properties against fire. Storm would have followed naturally, on these ferocious seas, and after that the fertility of potatoes. Food, fire and storm had always been the main measures of life for the islanders. Could a new form of pirate, centuries later, Taidhg or Seúinín, privateer or revenue man or raider from Achill, have been the one who smashed it up with a sledge-hammer, to stop its influence on the weather? Then came the thongs and flannel to keep it together: then the derogatory clergymen Otway and Nangle to mock it, and the priest O'Reilly to scotch the cause of scandal in the sea. When Canon O'Reilly caused them to fish it out again, a few yards from Carraigín dubh, the Black Rock — and a black day it must have been when they were made to throw it thence — he had found only a *pedestal*. If this 'pedestal' was really the little saint's pillow, more than a millennium old, I doubt whether the well-meaning canon was really allowed to impound it or to take it to the Dublin Museum. If the islanders of the 1870s resembled their descendants in simplicity, subtlety and natural piety: and if they knew, as they did know, and as Miss Cronin knew, that their naomhóg was a genuine object of Christian veneration: and if they had already retrieved and repaired it twice or three times: then surely, if that canon did go away with a stone, it was *any* stone, to keep his reverence happy, and their naoṁóg itself is probably back again today — I hope so — in its proper niche behind the lobster pots of Padden's cottage.

Incidentally, it has kept the cottage roofed and habitable.

In 1945, some years after the end of this story, Mlle Henry, the excavator of Inniskea, published her findings. She made no mention of the Godstone and did not seem to have heard of it, but she quoted from Adamnan's Life to the effect that a certain Cormac, grandson of Lethan and disciple of St Columba, once sailed from the region called Eirros Domno to seek a 'solitude in the ocean.'

Of her own finds she wrote: 'Both in Houses A and C[1] there were, lying on both sides of the 'bed-posts'', at the head of the sleeping space, two pebbles of red[2] stone about 10 ins. to 1 ft. long, egg-shaped and polished, most probably by the action of the sea. Their presence is certainly not accidental, but what was their function? Two possible explanations occur to me. They may have been primitive foot-warmers ... but ... such a sybaritical notion is hardly consistent with the atmosphere of early Irish monasteries ... Another solution lies in the suggestion that these stones were ascetics' pillows. There is for that hypothesis a very interesting analogy, that of a stone of about the same shape as the Inishkea ones, also a sea-pebble but about twice as big, which is at present preserved in the Cathedral of Iona. It was found lying on the ground within twenty yards of the large granite boulder beneath which, according to tradition, St Columba was buried. Commenting upon it,

[1] Beehive houses.
[2] Mrs Padden had said it was red.   Notice also the sizes given and the statements about polishing.

Joseph Anderson called attention to the passage of Adamnan's Life of St Columba where the death of the saint is described: " ... he returns to his cell, and sits up throughout the night on his bed, where he had the bare rock for pallet, and a stone for pillow which to this day stands by his grave as his monumental pillar." The stone has a cross carved on it, and the identification seems quite plausible. There is another stone of the same type but of unknown origin in the Cathedral of Iona; it is nearly as big as the first one and has a cross with expanded arms carved on it. St Ciaran, apparently, had a similar stone pillow. It is mentioned in his Irish Life, but the reference to it is much more elaborate in the Latin Life:

St Kiaranus used greatly to crucify his body, and we write here an example of this. He even had a stone pillow beneath his head, which, till today, remains in the monastery of St Kiaranus, and is reverenced by every one. Moreover, when he was growing weak he would not have the stone removed from him, but commanded it to be placed to his shoulders, that he should have affliction to the end for the sake of an everlasting reward in heaven.'

Bathing on summer days in the lace-work of the Atlantic rollers, frothy like milk just spurted in the pail, or stretched among the snail-shells on the sand dunes of Drumreagh, I often thought kindly of St Cormac or whoever he may have been, with his solitude and holy head-rest. His islands of repose stood lonely in the distance, their hazy silhouette topped by the sea-mark of the south one — a finger pointing to the heaven he had longed for. I never went to the islands again. For all I know, his skull still rolls in the golden sand, rewarded with his own kind of peace which passed all understanding, and as contented to be pillowed there, as it was with its godstone when living.[1]

[1] It only dawned on me while correcting the proofs of this chapter, that ⲛⲁⲟⲙⲟⲥ may actually *mean* a pillow. At least it does mean a 'cot', and we still *cradle* our heads on pillows.

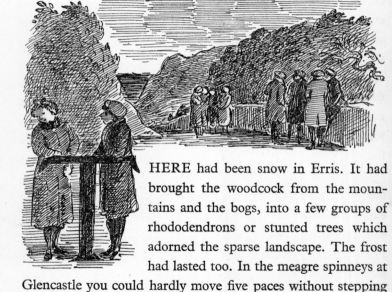

HERE had been snow in Erris. It had brought the woodcock from the mountains and the bogs, into a few groups of rhododendrons or stunted trees which adorned the sparse landscape. The frost had lasted too. In the meagre spinneys at Glencastle you could hardly move five paces without stepping on a small, dead bundle of fluffed feathers, weighing a gramme or two.

It was a Sunday evening, and Jack and I were sitting in the car on the Glen road, eating sandwiches. We had been driving over

136

a wide area, from covert to covert, where we had shot six snipe and eight and a half brace of woodcock. This was a lot of cock for one afternoon, so we were pleased. But, since we were fairly good shots, we were also slightly cross with each other for missing some of them. I was also feeling a little relieved that my setter was still alive. The technique for shooting these birds in those parts was to put the wildest dog you could find into a clump of rhododendrons and then shoot very quickly at whatever came out, in whatever direction. The setter was the one who stood in most peril from this manoeuvre. I had had the whole rhyme about 'never, never let your gun' spanked into me at an early age, but I doubted whether Jack had. You had to rely on the excellence of his aim, and also on the fact that his boundless good-nature generally took him into the bushes, along with the wild dog, to create a commotion — which often prevented him from shooting.

Glencastle was several miles from the village, but it was the nearest thing approaching a wood. On Sunday afternoons the adolescents of the district would congregate there for a strange, shy, stilted mating-ceremony, which was anything but sexual. For at least an hour the two genders would lean against the walls in separate flocks, the boys about fifty yards from the girls and mostly silent. Then one boy would approach one girl and lead her off with awkward gallantry, for a promenade among the short trees. They might as well have been storks, or courting peacocks, shy of their feet. If they ever got as far as holding hands, I should be surprised to hear of it. They seemed more likely to present each other with twigs or stones, laying them before one another with hopeful beaks. It was pretty.

The sexual life of Mayo amazed me, but I tried to believe what I was told. Seán gave me several lectures. The difference between Gael and Gall, he said, was in the temperature of the blood. No Gael could understand cold-blooded sin. He could understand rape or murder or any spontaneous ferocity — indeed, rather to my disgust, one of the heroes of the west was famous for suddenly having bitten off an Englishwoman's nose — but to him it was inconceivable that a man should coolly say, 'I will keep a mistress,' and do so. It was the English who did this, the logical, dispassionate nation of shop-keepers. The Irish might conceivably violate a woman, but they would never keep her. And, said Glynn, the crofter in whose cottage I was so often welcomed with tea not only did not sleep with his neighbour's wife, but did not think of her nor even entertain the idea. Seán asserted positively that masturbation happened only between the ages of sixteen and twenty — and this, in a countryside where economic necessity often kept men un-married until their fifties. That was why the Irish branch of the Catholic Church had a monomania on the subject of sex. The rarity of sexual sins mentioned at confession made them stand out in the priest's mind, gave them a scarcity value such as the phalarope has for the ornithologist, and consequently made them important.

Could it be that the Irish were more feminine than the English — frigider, less logical, less given to constructive fantasy?

Whatever the explanation, the boys at Glencastle were chaste.

And yet, Jack now told me as we munched our sandwiches and watched the innocent, speechless ceremony, one of the priests of this district had been accustomed to drive out on Sundays, actually with a stick, to disperse the gatherings. When he found a boy and a girl together, he would whack the boy and snatch the girl's hat and decamp with it. As it was generally her only hat, she had to go to the presbytery to ask for it, and take her scolding.

How unlike, observed Jack, this attitude was to the conduct of Donald Doolwee and his wife — two Viking giants who had once lived in this very glen.

Donald Doolwee?

Why, yes. Did I not know that they had a castle here? That was why it was called Glencastle. There were the remains of it on that hill in front of us, where we had been shooting, built to defend the pass. He had several other castles along Broadhaven.

Well?

Oh, well, said Jack, this Donald Doolwee had a war with another giant who had invaded his fiefs, and finally he got driven into the castle there, where he was besieged. It was a strong fort on a steep hill-top, as you see, and the other giant could not get him out. The siege went on for many years, until one day Donald's wife, the ogress, looked over the castle wall and saw the besieger. He had flaxen hair. Hers was black and her eyes were grey.

They looked upon one another steadfastly, and that was that.

Well now, this Donald Doolwee I was telling you about, he had a secret of his strength. One time there was a witch on Inniskea called Morna, whom he had loved. She had given him a hank of her hair to tie about his loins, and, while he had this lock about him, he was invincible. That was why the other giant could not get into the castle. Everybody knew he had some piseóg, but nobody knew what it was.

So, when the ogress had looked upon the other ogre, she went out to him over the wall, and they held one another. She promised to find out for him what the secret of her husband's might was.

She went on at Donald night and day from that time forth, until at last he produced a skull. He made her put her hand on this skull and swear by terrible oaths against her soul and body that she would not betray his secret if he revealed it to her. She swore, and he did reveal it, and she did betray. She cut away that hank of hair, and the flaxen-headed giant captured the castle, and Donald Doolwee was slaughtered in his blood.

They cut off his head and rolled it down the steep side of the dun — just there were the woodcock rolled, you remember, the one which Brownie found for us.

Then the wicked giantess went off with her fancy ogre according to his promise, Mr White, but little good did it do her. He knew her value, I can tell you! He drowned her next day in the Munhin river which flows out of Carrowmore, and her soul flapped away in the shape of a crane, shrieking for Revenge. It flew to Inniskea.

But, good God, Jack, I exclaimed: this is the fated crane of Inniskea, which I know all about because of those searches for the Godstone, and which we saw hoisting herself across the ocean with her reflection flying under her, upside down, and which was probably the Thing Which Brayed that flew up under my feet in the darkness when I was alone to shoot the barnacles — and wait — oh listen! I think I can quote you some Latin about her from O'Flaherty's *Ogygia*.

> Insulâ Iniskeâ, Scriptis ut fama priorum
> Credula commendat, regis qua prominet Irras
> Oceani in fluctus, grus est ab origine rerum
> Unica Syderibus minime consumpta coaevis.

Well, God help ye, Mr White, said Jack, impressed, with that head of yours!

Listen, it means more or less this:

There is a crane or heron in the island of Inniskea — so the credible tradition in writings of the ancients tells us — I mean that region where Erris sticks out into the billows of the ocean — and this crane has been there since the beginning of things. It is the only one of its kind, eternal with the eternal stars.

If it was that crane of Donald Doolwee's, it could not have been there since the beginning of things, said Jack.

But I was too far flown by now to listen to any objections.

Jack, I can give you another verse out of *Ogygia*. Listen now:

Cernere Inisgloriâ est pelago, quod prospicit Irras
Insulâ avos, at avosque solo post fata Sepultos
Effigies servare suas, vegetisque vigere
Unguibus, atque comis. Hominum caro nulla putrescit.

Well, then?

Jack had no objection to my talking Latin, enjoyed the noise, believed in my enthusiasms, and knew I was not showing off.

It is this, I said. I have probably got it wrong. I only have the 1685 edition. I don't know whom he was quoting — if he was quoting — and I think the accents or punctuation may be misprinted in it. Anyway I don't understand Latin much. But it's this, more or less:

In the sea which Erris looks across, there is to be seen an island called Inisgloria. In it, they say that grandfathers and great-grandfathers, once they are dead and buried, preserve their forms and remain quick, with growing hair and nails. No human flesh putrifies.

Well, said Jack, everybody knows and always has known that corpses do not corrupt on Innislgora. Why do you suppose that St Brendan was still there and his wooden statue in the beehive cell? Or was it St Molaise?

But, Jack, I don't know these things. I am supposed to be a Protestant. You must be merciful to my ignorance and explain about them.

It is possible to walk out to Inniglora, he said patiently, but only at the lowest springs, and no woman must go there. It is perfectly true that corpses do not corrupt in the peat-soil of the island, which is acid, like tannin, and no scientist has ever disputed this simple fact. You know yourself of the church in Dublin where you can put your finger into the leathery wound of a crusader. They give me to understand that some herdsman or other of the Stone Ages was lately dug up in Sweden or some place, and the peat had preserved the weave of his garments. Besides this, what about that east-coast butcher who murdered his brother and buried the joints in a bog, only to have them dug up again and reassembled, in perfect preservation?

But, Jack...

All that is of no importance. Anybody can prove it. The interesting thing is that no woman may go to Innisglora.

Well, it was a monastery. Perhaps it was St Brendan's monastery...

Look, my good man, said he, laying his hand on my thigh in the motor-car, if you go to Inniglora as a male, you will find that bodies are imperishable. Rats — but not mice — can live there, and earth from the island will banish them from your house if taken to the mainland.[1] In 1841, he added, rather startling me because I thought I was the only person who was interested in dates, there was a saint's beehive there, in fine preservation. You can still see the ruin. People who entered his

[1] Jack could not possibly have known that rats were a late importation into Europe. Rats, like cats, came in historic times. In medieval bestiaries, there were few cats, some mice, no rats, But there were mice. And the ancient anecdotes talked about the *mice* of Innisglora.

igloo had to take bread with them. Each, holding the piece of bread in his right hand, had to break the bread and eat it. They could only be males.

In that monastic island of Innisglora, from which the discoverer of America was said to have come, about eight centuries before Columbus, it was true that women were not admitted. There was a well there. If a woman drew water from this well, it turned blood red and was full of scarlet worms. When their menfolk were away from the island, fishing, there was only one thing to do. The woman could draw the water, but she then had to hand it to any little boy. He, although his virility was not mature, could make it right by touching the bucket.

Driving home rather silently, through the shy boys and more frigid girls, I wondered about the West.

You came there with scientific prejudices against fairies and against the claptrap of the Dublin poeticals — and the inhabitants patiently repeated their legends. There really was a Fairy Fire, which I had seen and indeed licked with my own physical tongue. There really was a naomhóg, a minor deity who turned out to be the pillow of a Christian hermit. There really was an island, just as O'Flaherty and indeed Giraldus in the twelfth century had related, where bodies did not decay because of some property in the soil, and where women were not welcome — because it had been a monastery. Here was a vast complex of traditional history, much richer than anything remembered by the English prior to 1066, and something real always seemed to turn up under the legend.

Why not bring some earth from Innisglora, and try it on rodents? D.D.T. would have been a magic powder a few years ago, and penicillin a disgusting and superstitious mould. Were there red worms in the well? What did Innisglora mean? Who was the chief saint originally famous on this system of islets—Brendan, Cormac, Kay, or all of them? Had there been a nunnery on South Inniskea to match the monasteries to the north? It was marked on Ordnance Survey, just as Glencastle was. And if Glencastle were real, why not Donald Doolwee—and whence came his garbled name? His fort, Glencastle, really had been called Dundonnell in the sixteenth century. And if Donald were real, why not his wife, the fated crane who cried Revenge, and what connection had she with the witch Morna of the naomhóg island?

One of the commonest birds in the waters of Inniskea was the shag or perhaps cormorant, whose Gaelic name was cailleach-dubh — the Black Hag.

What, in short, was the link between Grus, the crane—which is now the Irish name for the heron—and Inniskea, where, by day and night, you still came across the modern version of these birds? Could the island have been on a route of some migration?

To my shame, I never did collect any of the soil to banish mice. But I did chase the Grus through medieval bestiaries, which date back to the fifth century.

The only immortal birds known to ancient naturalists were the Eagle and the Phoenix. Both had a faint plausibility for

Erris. Eagles had once been common there, just as the chough was still to be found — and the Phoenix, it is strange to relate, may well have been the Purple Heron. All over Ireland, herons are called cranes.

An immortal heron, crane or stork — immortal since she was always seen to return on migration, but never to breed, as indeed the sunbird did to Heliopolis — might well have fitted with the phoenix, half-remembered by some learned monk in this country district where the peasants were notoriously confused in their local bird names. The 'Grus' itself, according to the bestiarists, was a great migrator. If Donald's wife, that faithless sentinel, had been forced to emigrate, and if there had been some ancient route of 'Grus'-migration through the islands, perhaps she might have betaken herself to Inniskea?

Country people are as bad at ornithology as they are at history. Phoenices can turn into storks or cranes or herons as easily as Viking pirates or Norman invaders can turn into giants — as easily, in fact, as the crane has already turned into the heron, for the Irish. If these two, why not the similar stork also, and was there ever a stork route up the west coast of Ireland?

The bestiarists are nearly as bad as the country people, and you are never perfectly certain that you are rightly translating Ciconia, Grus and Ardea as Stork, Crane and Heron. Incidentally, Ardea ought to have something to do with 'ardeo', burning up — and there we were again, back with the Phoenix, who used to burn herself up at Heliopolis.

146

There was one other migratory bird in the bestiaries who might have had slight affinities with witches and fated 'cranes'. This was Coturnix, the Quail. She lived on poisonous seed, for which reason the ancients forbade her to be eaten, and she was the only other animal which suffers from the falling sickness like man'.

I mentioned the falling sickness to Jack, who said: But does it not be known to everybody that you can make a crane (heron) faint by stalking her? If you can creep up on a crane without her seeing you, and jump up with a shout close by, she will fall in a fit.

Good gracious, said I, I have done it myself without realizing what I was doing! I stalked a heron once and gave her one barrel, and she fell down, but then she got up again and I had to give her another. I wish I had not shot that heron. Such a beautiful lemon eye, and her wet bill, and her exquisite, ruffled, untidy grey hackles. It was pure ferocity, Jack, needless and beastly. One day I shall have to give up shooting altogether.

GOT out of the bus in a bad temper — bored, exhausted, and angry about being driven across Ireland in these bloody vehicles, which had remarks written on them in Gaelic that nobody could understand. Korus Umpar Airan: that was what it sounded like. Ridiculous. And Ireland, the once individualistic place, which of all places ought not to be nationalized, had turned its transport over to

148

the Farewell State of Mr De Valera. 'Farewell, a long farewell to all my greatness.'

But damn the Nationalists for making me change at half a hundred stops, as it seemed — for writing Telefon on telephone boxes which could just as well have been described in the words of the Italian who invented them — and, more than all, and even more unreasonably, double-damn them for making me bring these two untrained shooting dogs a couple of hundred miles. I had a setter and a pointer, and they had to be taught shooting. Both had been sick more than once, and we were not welcome in nationalized conveyances, and we had had to suck up to ten thousand bus-conductors for mere tolerance. The thing was to get the dogs to be sick on the step of the bus. Some conductors could put up with this. Some could not. Through Mullingar, through the various bishoprics, we had pressed on, with bloody, green-hatted energy. My less rabid companion in the journey was a schoolmaster from the east.

This teacher or ollamh, who had taught me whatever I knew of his beautiful but infuriating language, was a real person. He was a short, determined master — a teaching man, who had somehow married a bird-like woman, who might have been a ballet dancer. His wife once told me that, if he drank a dram too much of whisky, his heart would actually throb the bed. His heart, like a bird's, really shook his frame, and so it did hers, and so did hers his. They were two angels who had got married. It might have been Toscanini who had married some famous duchess from Knowle.

He got out of the bus behind me and watched with amusement, while I fussed with bags and baggage. It was night by now, and the vehicle took itself off, diminishing across the boundless turf and under the boundless skies of Mayo, burrowing along in its own cocoon of light between the two, until its bright windows were only a glow-worm of the vasty moorland — but still full of women from market and drunk farmers and black shawls and untidy parcels, all of which I equally loathed for the time being. As a matter of fact, the deeper we had got into the lovely province, the more we had been recognized by friend after friend, the less the busmen had persecuted us, and the better we had been teased or quizzed or welcomed, until the final conductor had practically been tugging my famous whiskers, in good-humour and warmth of heart.

I was in no mood for all this. Many months in the east, among the fillers-up-of-forms, had reduced me to the natural meanness of civilization. I was convinced that we had caught the wrong connection at Mullingar, lost our cartridges or guns at Ballina, been robbed somewhere intermediately, and probably had not got the right kind of ration books or passports or identity cards or dog licences or shooting permits or practically anything else for where we were meant to be. Those months had made me forget that the body can't be nourished on bits of paper. I had forgotten that man only needs water, food, fire and sleep — in that order — none of which are well represented by printed forms. I had forgotten that in the west this fact was remembered. Also, I had forgotten that if you were robbed, you were robbed. The world did not come to an end because you were. And the incidence of larceny at Piccadilly Circus was about five thousand per cent higher than it was anywhere west of Ballina.

Séamus O'Flynn, the teacher who was taking a fortnight's holiday at my shooting-lodge to help with the dogs, for he was a passionate shooter and trainer of animals too, examined my gyrations with sympathetic amusement. I had been bullying him for the last fifty miles, about where the cartridges were. He knew they were either where they were, or else they were not. He came from the south of Ireland. Although he did not quite share the same blás, he did share the same culture as the western Gael. He looked down upon me with a friendly smile, though his eyes were about on a physical level with my chin, rather as the giant Gulliver must have examined the Lilliputians.

Incidentally, in the troubles, Séamus had been on the run. He had been chased by the race and policy then represented and still represented by me. His life had been in his own hands then, and in the hands of his compatriots. I disagreed with his political views, as he disagreed with mine. We kept a neutrality of esteem on these subjects. I think he would have shot me, if he had been told to do so by Authority — because he was a Catholic, and therefore conditioned to accept orders.

I do not think that anything would have persuaded me to shoot Séamus, because I had been brought up as a Protestant, to protest against authority. I might, as an armed guard detailed to take him away and execute him, have said: Well, run, you ass, while I pretend to do up my bootlace. But I would not have given him this law, I admit, if there had been a sergeant watching, who could shoot me for sparing Séamus.

These heart-searchings were getting us no farther towards solving the situation in the now ill-lit hamlet — the bus had been the main illumination — in which I was dashing about, like a cockchafer in a hat box, proclaiming that the imaginary skis and the pemmican and the snow-glasses and the pitons and the important parts of the oxygen apparatus and the infra-red camera and every single file of the card-index had been lost, stolen or strayed, so that we should never get up my mental Everest.

Some amused silence on the part of the observers must have brought me to my senses, for I looked up at last. There was Cathal Barrett standing in the light of the grocer's window — where he had been taking a glass of whisky while waiting to meet us. He was a wiry fellow of sixty or more, with a drooping blond moustache and faded blue eyes, out of which he regarded me with the wonderful, polite, protective attention which only the best ghillies in Scotland can offer to their lairds.

He had taken over both dogs the moment we alighted, and was holding them on tight leads, so that their forelegs were almost on tiptoe with immobility. This maddened me still further. The Irish, I thought: barbarians: cruel to animals! As a matter of fact, it was far the best way to hold headstrong puppies — who, if allowed a long leash simply throttle their windpipes on the end of it, while, if they are only given an inch

or two, they support their jaw-bones on the collar. It was to be
at least ten days before it dawned on me that Cathal had been
handling setters when my own nannie was handling safety pins.

I took the dogs from him insultingly, signifying that, robbed
and benighted as I was, I was ready to mount the local taxi
— which he had hired for us — with what remained of our
luggage.

As to the luggage — what a good word 'luggage' is, by the
way: we had *lugged* it across Ireland — the few pieces not there
at the time were delivered, without charge, before breakfast
next morning.

We ascended the taxi.

Five miles farther into the bog, wedged together with dogs
and gunboxes and the faintly anxious-looking Cathal — he was
anxious not to be rude to me in return for my rudeness — our
headlights turned to the right through a broken gateway into a
tunnel of overgrown rhododendrons: and into, precisely, the
year 1889.

In Guernsey, in the Channel Islands, the City of Paris has
preserved Victor Hugo's ridiculous home exactly as he pompously left it. For a small fee, it is possible to enter the house and
to have the uneasy feeling that, at any moment, the old gentleman may open the front door with his own key, stump upstairs
smelling faintly of tobacco, and sit down on his water-closet —
which has blue cabbage roses on the enormous bowl, and the

The sitting room at Glen Affran

sort of piston which you have to pull upwards in a cataract of Hugo-like noises.

Glenaffron Lodge was like this, and for good reason.

In 1889, when Cathal Barrett was scarcely born, its absentee landlords had walked out of it, perhaps because of some minor unpleasantness about being shot by the locals, and they had never come back. For all anybody seemed to know, they might have become extinct — though their heirs and assignees did have a solicitor somewhere in Kent, from whom I had hired the mansion.

Cathal's parents and he himself had, since that momentous day, farmed the land and studiously inhabited only the kitchen, dusting the other rooms fairly often, preserving everything *in situ* — against the never-coming day of the master's return.

How glorious, in the era of atomic weapons and of proximity fuses, to be able to step straight into a Smoking Room of the 'nineties, dank and musty, with mildewed leather fringes on the bookshelves, and to pick up the calabash pipe set down by some indignant sportsman in a Norfolk jacket and spats, his backside still tingling from the traditional charge of buckshot inflicted by the tenantry! There, on the round mahogany table, was the very latest number of the *Strand Magazine* with the globe of its street-lamp on the cover. There, for the more high-brow ladies, if I am not getting my dates mixed, was an *avant-garde* periodical calling itself *The Nineteenth Century*, and in it — could it have been? — an article by some subaltern called Churchill or by the new writer Kipling. The smoking-cap, unless this is an exaggeration, hung on the door, Certainly the deer-stalker hung in the hall, among the antlers. In the female bed-rooms there were curling tongs and rolls of false hair and red books with their covers licked, in lieu of rouge, and bits of rice paper for face powder. In the male bedrooms there were cycling breeches and dancing pumps, with bows on them, and cut-throat razors marked for the days of the week. Yes, and there was a half-empty bottle of Rowland's Macassar Oil, still sporting its astonishing list of patrons.

The advertisements in the magazines were entrancing. In

blacker ink than we now have, on shinier paper, they displayed babies reaching for cakes of soap out of hip baths, cones or pyramids of some mysterious substance which could be ignited against asthma, ladies in bloomers leaning on bicycles, dress-makers' busts with knobs instead of heads and cages instead of legs and undivided bosoms leaning forward. The illustrations of the stories were engraved with wonderful detail, showing coy maidens with masses of high hair being grasped in moonlit woods by inhibited gentlemen in high collars. In the Irish stories there were fairies here and there, with dragon-fly wings and toadstools and bits of shamrock and plenty of jolly Paddies leading pigs on strings. By the way, what an excellent word 'shamrock' is too: its first syllable is definitive. Nobody in the west cared a fig about its symbolism.

Then there were ancient salmon flies in the drawers, with eyes of gut, now unreliable, and bushy hackles, but still recogniz-able as Jock Scotts or Alexandras — and machines for turning over the tops of cartridges or measuring their charges — and heavy, wooden reels with brass fittings — and glove-stretchers of ivory, with tarnished, silver-topped bottles — and a letter or two from Tommy at Simla — and a dance programme with its white pencil still attached — and a game-book in which some-body had defiantly entered $3\frac{1}{2}$ brace of grouse.

In the drawing-room there were fans and peacock feathers and pampas grass.

Among the kerosene lamps and plush chairs, and table cloths with bobbles on them, and stereoscopic holders for viewing three-dimensional pictures of the Sphinx, and stuffed pheasants, and moth balls, and albums with clasps, and carriage whips, and enormous hats with sea-gulls transfixed by jet hatpins, and boot-trees, and dangerous engines for making aerated water, and little flower vases for button holes, and golf balls of gutta-percha and a cleek — among these — since it was Ireland — there were inevitably two or three pieces of eighteenth-century silver, candlesticks and such like, with good cut-glass and several empty bottles of claret.

Over everything there was a microscopic film of dust.

So forgotten, so lost, so distant, so remote from shops was this blissful abode of peace that the Barretts had killed a skeep for our provision. And this, without a refrigertator, we were gradually to consume from top to toe during the next fortnight of summer weather.

Yes, the word was sanctum or sanctuary. Into this sanctum, Cathal ushered us with deference — by the soft light of an oil lamp with a smoked chimney.

He was a man, we slowly discovered, who was as singular as the house which he inhabited. He was a poet.

There is a secret world of literature, unknown to professional writers and even to collectors of folklore, which covers the globe in an infinitely thin veneer. All the people in this coating know each other, but are unknown outside the layer.

They publish their works in the back pages of *Old Moore's Almanack*.

From Chicago to Calcutta to Cork, under signatures or initials or names of the pen, 'Erin Go Braw' addresses his melodious rhymes to P.J.W., while Evan Williams tunes a note of exhortation to 'Aussie Boy'. Their subjects are Spring, Moonlight, Patriotism, Colleens, Mother Love, or the merits of one another. They often set versified riddles or anagrams or conundrums. Their interests are studious, their craftsmanship complicated, their minds similar to those of chess-players, and their courtesy — if sometimes inclined to a learned dig or leg-pull — invariably above suspicion. Presumably they are lonely people, with infinite leisure, living in lighthouses and weather-ships and wigwams and igloos and Irish bogs, looking forward to the publication of next year's *Old Moore*, doing all the puzzles of this year, inventing the most subtle diversions and 'cracks' and 'teazers', with which to encourage, improve, reprove or entertain their friends.

Cathal was one of them.

He was one of the chief bards of the *Almanack*. He frequently set a conundrum to 'Semper Fidelis' in the Antipodes, was locally famous and spoken of with awe for having appeared in print, and he was certain that I, as a professional writer, would make fun of him. I do not mean to do so. It is difficult to rise to the top of any profession, and, the more recondite the profession is, the greater the competition. If I have any claim to be the equal of Cathal, it is that I, in open struggle, heat after heat, on Radio Eireann, was once acclaimed the leading Bard of Erin myself, and was awarded more than one prize of five shillings.

The chastity of the Irish is a subject which never ceases to baffle the Anglo-Saxon. Perhaps they mature later, perhaps it has something to do with their very ancient cenobitic form of Christianity, perhaps there is an economic reason tied up with the poverty of small, unfruitful farms — but the fact is that the Gael marries late. It is difficult in the modern world to imagine people who do not divorce one another and who wait to be married until they are fully grown — indeed, until they are middled-aged. Perhaps it is because they mate for life, and expect to be continent and faithful, that they marry so slowly and with such precaution. Perhaps also the occasional violence of the Irish — their eruptions — may be due to repression of the carnal instincts.

Until they are wedded, the menfolk of Mayo are called 'boys'. Cathal had remained a boy until the last decade of his life.

Imagine that lifetime on the heathery mountains, and the keen eyes once brilliantly blue, missing no movement of sheep or cattle, wild goose or hare, hawk or infrequent neighbour. What secret longings must Cathal have had, what thwarted and complicated puzzles or day-dreams, as he shepherded on the high shoulders of Slieve Fyagh in the lonely sunlight? He was noticeably gentle with animals. He had held the dogs that evening on the short leash to help them, not to punish. To beat a shooting dog — and this was rare among keepers — would have struck him as madness. For forty-five years, since the beginning of manhood, he had loitered above Glenaffron in rain or shine, often with his still hand on the dog's head which helped with his herding — patient, waiting for something, silent and watchful as the dog beside.

So there we were in this astonishing house, with its faithful and accomplished game-keeper, who had bided sixty years for his master to come home, and had dusted the calabash or meerschaum at least once a week. He was slightly on the defensive, could not quite make us out for not being cross about that charge of buckshot in his employer's trousers, knew perfectly well that I was a brighter light than he was in the literary world, and, while expecting the Saxon insult which he had every reason to foresee after our first meeting, he still watched me with grave and accommodating politeness — while I trained the setter and the pointer quite amiss. The most difficult thing in the world is to know how to do a thing, and to watch somebody else doing it wrong, without comment. Cathal managed it.

After nearly twenty years, now that I know better about dogs, I realize that he was training me, just as I thought myself to be training them.

But the point of this story is a love affair. It was over the course of more than one year that I finally discovered its features. He concealed them from me, with the sensitive reticence of the Gael, and I made no particular efforts to ferret them out.

Perhaps it was a commonplace in Mayo.

At one time, when over sixty and a bachelor, it had struck this sandy-moustached, moist-eyed bard and ghostly ghillie, that he was now in an economic position to get married.

So he had put into action the existing machinery.

He had sent for the local matchmaker, had provided him with a bottle of whisky to take away, and had stated his financial position with its possibilities. Leave you all to me, the matchmaker had said, for I have the very girl you need.

The matchmaker had then put the necessary bottle in his pocket, had walked across the mountain into the next glen, and had set the bottle on the table. Glens are as separate from one another as fjords are.

On sight of the matchmaker and the bottle, which had not to be broached until the decent moment, the daughter of the house, a strong and pretty girl about eighteen, had been sent out to count the chickens. It had been stated, after ceremonious nuances, that Cathal had such and such assets, while the girl herself might expect in dowry a pig and a cow. The bottle had then been uncorked.

Cathal, over sixty, met his bride, under twenty, for the first time, actually at the altar where they were married.

A deplorable state of affairs!

The only trouble about it was that my schoolmaster and myself were a bit of a bore to the Barretts, during our harvest stay, eating the putrefying sheep. They could never be sure of being alone together, and, however tactful we were about absenting ourselves on mountains or coughing when approaching their small hay-field, they had too little time, what with suckling the happy babies and dodging behind the haycocks for another heart-warming hug, to attend to the less lovely and gentle duties of hospitality.

CHARLIE PLUNKETT was on the far side of middle age, but he was not elderly yet. Soon after his marriage — which had taken place many years before — he had found that he detested his wife and that she detested him. So he had given her all his possessions, had shaken the domestic dust of Erris from his feet — or rather the sand of it — and had taken ship for Australia. He had been there more than thirty years.

For thirty years he had knocked about the good-on continent

163

as an engineer or something of that sort — picking up a little money here and there, solitary, self-sufficient, not complaining out loud. He had a mathematical mind — the kind that engineers do have — with which he pondered useless statistics, such as the population of New South Wales or the circumference of the globe at the equator or the distance to the moon and the tonnage of ships. He did not rant about his wife, and, being a good Catholic, he did not seek to replace her. He was a silent, enduring, patient fellow, obviously in need of love or friendship. He was a bit of a bore. I thought he must once have loved his wife a great deal. Where women were concerned, he gave the impression of being drained or exhausted, like a hospital patient who had given up the effort to be convalescent. But he made no bids for sympathy. In fact, he tried to conceal his loneliness. Often, when he longed to talk to me about Australia or shipping companies or the distance to the moon, I could see him check himself. He spent a lot of time wandering on the sandy beaches, a sole figure in the distance, collecting something. We never knew what.

Among the fortune-seekers of the Antipodes, he may have been a failure. Among his neighbours of Erris, he was a minor success. For he had saved enough money to live on — just enough — and he had returned to his birthplace. He was boarding at his sister's cottage — a few miles from the wife of whom he still spoke neither good nor ill — while he looked about him for a cottage of his own. People do tend to go back to their beginnings when they are ready to die.

A NEW BOY IN THE SCHOOL OF DEATH

A wise man once said that all the middle-aged people in the world are living lives of quiet desperation. My own life was difficult enough to carry forward, without the encumbrance of a stranger's troubles. I tried to give him a little of the company he pined for — but we both knew that, if we went too far, he would clamp himself on my shoulders like the Old Man of the Sea. So we rationed our meetings, as it were, by common consent. Once or twice a week I listened for an hour or two to his 'yarns' about waltzing Matildas. At other times, he was careful not to take advantage.

We took him to Inniskea that day in the motor-boat, for the jaunt, and he was pleased and excited. He even became voluble, and told, almost vauntingly, a long, dull story about some wallabies.

He always walked slowly. I was trying to bustle him from St Columba's tiny church up the slope of the Bailey mór, when he turned pale and stopped altogether. He explained that he had a weak heart. I was involved in my own excitements about the antiquities of the island and was impatient with him. He looked healthy enough to me, was by no means an old man, and I suppose I was for the time being a little tired of being used by him as a source of sympathy — however carefully he did it. So we sat him down on a stone wall to rest — since the shell-mound of loose sand was obviously too steep for him to conquer — and we scrambled up the incline by ourselves. Afterwards, we collected him from the wall on which he had been sitting and panting, and I remember feeling disappointed in him, or perhaps reproachful. I felt that he had stupidly missed a great treat, by not climbing up to see those ancient grave-stones and the prehistoric igloos. He did not talk in the boat on the way home.

A week later, Mr Plunkett sat up in bed at 4 a.m., wearing his night-shirt, swung his legs over the side, put on his trousers, and died.

Jack of the Garage took me to the wake. It would have been hateful to go as a tripper from curiosity, but we had known him personally — had been, I suppose, not quite unkind to him — and I felt a compassion for this spent life, its solitude patiently borne. Jack said that it would not only be right for us to go there, but wrong not to go.

The cottage, at which we arrived on foot in the evening, was like most of the others in Erris. A handful of rather tatterdemalion figures in dark serge — the women with black shawls over their heads — were drifting towards or round its not recently whitewashed walls. The thatched roof had been replaced by corrugated iron. Jack whispered instructions about what we ought to do.

We went into the little porch, to be welcomed solemnly by the sister in mourning, with whom we shook hands. There seemed to be three or four rooms in the house, which was bigger than many. He was in the front room.

We knelt beside the coffin to say the expected prayer, glancing fearfully at the wax face, in whose nostrils the stiff hair looked blacker than in life. The pinched nose was arrogant and stilly, bleak with the cool contempt of death. He had covered the whole distance from alpha to omega — was in this great matter more experienced than any of us.

The room stretched up to the rafters, without a ceiling. At one end, the embrasure for the turf fire was deep enough to hold an ingle seat. There were tins of tea or other groceries on the high shelf. The coffin stood along the inner wall, its lid upright at the head of it, lit by three candles in a branched candlestick. Two cheap religious prints and a plaster statuette of the Virgin Mary presided over it. Three benches or forms, such as one finds in poor schoolhouses, had been ranged on the opposite side of the room, facing the corpse. In front of them was a plain kitchen table, on which there lay a couple of dozen clay pipes already filled with shag. We fumbled our way to the hindmost bench and sat down reverently, to survey the company.

An old man was smoking in the ingle nook. Two women sat at the foot of the coffin with their shawls hiding their faces, so that they looked like nuns. On the benches in front of us, an assortment of fishermen with strong, individual expressions — one of them with the profile of Punch — sucked the blue shag-smoke through the new, suffocating pipes. We were given a clay each and offered porter or whisky, of which we chose whisky. As each newcomer came in, he knelt beside the coffin.

I was determined to behave with proper solemnity. So it was startling when the old man in the nook took the pipe out of his mouth and shouted some teasing quip about the weather to Jack. It was still more startling when the Punch-and-Judy figure and the old man fell to work, telling anecdotes about the scandalous adventures and the pretended sexual prowess of the deceased. Vulgar stories, jolly reminiscences, animated conversations on all kinds of subjects — so far as I can remember even secular songs — began to liven the assembly. I was surprised, if not shocked.

The point was, of course, that everybody was trying to amuse Charlie Plunkett.

Otherwise, why 'wake' him? We were there to give him company, support, help, love, during his first lost hours straying beside the body. That was why we were sitting up with him. Obviously the best possible treatment was to entertain him — to flatter him, to keep his heart up, to take his mind from his troubles — and this we did, for pity and protection, by means of song and vulgarity. We were clowning, to hearten Mr Plunkett. We were codding him along. We were there so that he should not be lonely and homesick as a new boy on his first night in the school of death.

In the last century, and perhaps at the beginning of this one, a wake lasted for two or three days, during which the poor tyro at dissolution was never left to suffer his novelty alone. On the second night, Jack said, the young men and maidens of the village played games in the room to keep him cheerful. Some of them were acting-games of great antiquity, in which the ferry boat of the Styx was acted out according to a traditional mode. Some were like Blindman's Buff or Forfeits. In one of them, each blindfold 'he' was slapped by a girl until he guessed her name. Earlier still, the wakes were said to have ended in something not unlike an orgy. On the third day, at the burial, the caoineadh which was pronounced 'keen' would be raised by hired women at the graveside — a howl of terrible poignancy, said Jack.

Nowadays, the coffin went to the chapel after the first night, and there it was left alone. Presumably this was to prevent the orgies. It seemed to me a colder and less compassionate way of doing things.

When Mr Plunkett had spent his second night in solitude on holy ground — the sharp, disdainful nose, battened down by the coffin lid, silently expressing his valuation of life as a completed whole — his neighbours carried him on their shoulders to the grave.

Some of the graveyards of Erris, like many others in Eire, were shocking from an Anglo-Saxon point of view. They were Shakespearian — suitable for Yorick. Tombs which were above ground might have their sides broken. On those below, the earth might have caved. Shattered coffins, scattered thigh bones or skulls coloured like the soil which had held them, were common objects. At Termoncarragh there was a box-like sepulchre whose lid had fallen off. The coffins inside had rotted

A funeral in Erris

away and the two skeletons lay side by side — their faces turned towards each other in touching companionship. Rabbit burrows communicated with the dead. In one of the graves, half full of drifted sand, there was only a mummified seagull. The matter of adipocere — which in the case of at least one hallowed cadaver in Mayo had once been collected and eaten as a medicine by sufferers from tuberculosis — was rather a horrible one.

Yet this attitude to death, after the first shock, was not repulsive.

It was the unbelievers who had to cosset their corpses with fireproof vaults of eternal concrete in Hollywood. They had nothing else to tend. For believers — and the peasants of Erris were absolute believers — it did not matter much what happened to the body, after the soul had been waked away to Purgatory. They could afford to leave the dry ribs in the rabbit holes nonchalantly, because the important part was under care elsewhere. The Irish Catholic, indeed, with his reliance on the hereafter, always was less concerned about death, bloodshed, war or murder than his English cousin, who secretly doubted the future life. Murder, to a Saxon, was the great sin: it took away the greatest thing he could think of, life. The Catholic Gael regarded murder only as an incident in the existence of the eternal spirit, which could not be destroyed. For him, adultery was the greatest sin, because it was dangerous to salvation.

So Mr Plunkett was carried shoulder-high to his clean, sandy lot in one of the tidier graveyards, while his handful of friends, but not his wife, followed silently behind. He went in, that Ulysses, that circumnavigator, that antipodean, that cheated husband, that diffident student of the distance to the moon. It was hardly a generous hand which life had dealt to him, poor digger. Many millions of sheep he must have seen, under many torrid suns, and drank many a billy-can of wood-smoked tea. What wood? Eucalyptus, blue gum? Anyway, trees: of which there were none in Erris. He had come from here, and come back here, broken-backed in the middle by the bitter words of a woman. Now, on his salty grave, there would be no flowers or vegetation, none of the green of New South Wales. The only ornaments on the sepulchres of Erris were round white stones, collected and lovingly placed there by remembering mourners — those, and always a cardboard boot-box, holding the clay pipes which had been smoked at the wake.

These were a proof, by their numbers, of how many people had liked him well enough to bear him company, during his first night of bewilderment.

They must have been valued by the ghosts of Erris, who may have taken precedence in a kind of pecking-order, by virtue of the number of pipes which they could claim. The chieftain ghosts, as they sat among the tumbled grave-stones sucking their clays with broken teeth at midnight, might often have shown two boxes full. Charlie Plunkett's box had few.

I WAS involved in some confusion with an octopus made of red pepper, when the dream tilted sideways in the brutal frenzy of the alarm clock.

The linoleum was icy. There was a skin of ice in the chamber pot. The garish, glaring, pitiless light of the electric bulb searched out the sparse, winter bedroom too brilliantly for gummed eyes — absolutely drunk with sleep. It

173

showed black night through the window glass. Fluff moved on the lino in the north wind under the door. The red setter, curled warmly on the foot of the bed, opened one optic upon me as I stumbled to the raving clock, hopping from mat to mat because of the freezing floor. She still had time for a few more winks.

I dressed with hasty fingers, fumbling the buttons, dashing the cold water from the wash basin on haggard eyes, hissing like a groom.

There was a Thermos in the empty eating room, which seemed debauched by memories of the previous evening. A chair was crooked, ash-trays were full, a motionless book lay face downward, untidy in the sterile light. The turf fire was a roué of tarnished ash. I put rum in the hot tea and munched unwanted biscuits, gradually coming alive. Actions till now automatic began to become logical and purposive.

Termoncarragh. I looked at the wrist-watch. Five-thirty. Yes, we would get there in plenty of time. The wind would be blowing down the lake. It was to be hoped that the car would start without a fuss.

In the early mornings, people are zombies. They obey themselves mechanically, performing what the other and reasoning mind has plotted to do before it went to sleep. My zombie was beginning to live.

I offered Brownie tea and biscuits, which she refused. I began to check, in the awakening brain, the numerous gadgets of the wildfowler — the cartridges of various loads and so forth.

The Jaguar, relieved of its rugs and radiator lamp, started at a touch. I clambered into it, hustled by the pleased dog, and the headlights created the cobbled yard, while the car's petrol pump continued to tick.

The mounting road towards Corclogh and Annagh was an unfrequented one at the best of times. In the hours before dawn it was desolation itself, running between turf walls. The lights wound it under the spool of the car bumpers, as I blew on mittened fingers to warm them up.

I was alive. I began to hug myself as usual, at the delight of being awake and living, while others of the western world were all asleep and dead. There was a stealthiness, a sense of power and virtue common to huntsmen and burglars. It was a silent glee. Every bit of my body was healthy and younger than it is now, alas, and tingling with superiority. I thought with pity or condescension of the sleeping bodies in the few cottages by the roadside, of the dull, defenceless, sparkless clay. They were wasting the glorious chance of life. Why did anybody ever sleep at all? Surely, if we were only to have seventy years of it, it would be better not to miss a minute? And yes, I thought, I could switch off this engine, and walk up your boithrín, my lads, seeing in the dark, and lift your latch with the silence of a panther and slit your leaden throats without a sound. The powerful world of night belonged to me.

Termoncarragh was one of the characteristic lakes of Erris. It stood towards the root of the peninsula called Kilmore, as

Termon Kilmore stood at the tip of it. 'Tearmann' meant a sanctuary, a place of security, a shelter. They were the boundary marks of the peninsula.

It was a private theory of mine that Erris, possibly the least known quarter of Ireland and the one with the smallest amount of documented history, had in the early days of Christianity been a vast eremitical sanctuary or diocese, possibly converted by a saint called Comán. The inland section of Erris, if one regarded it as having been converted from the sea, was called Kilcommon — surely the church or diocese of Comán, just as one speaks of the 'church' of Laodicea. The seaward section, that of the peninsula, was called Kilmore — the Great Church, using 'church' in the same sense. And the very node or seamost shrine of the mission was, I believed, then and now the island of Inniskea — the island of repose or retreat, in the religious meaning of the word. Probably St Comán had originally landed on or near the island from the sea, had extended his beachhead to include the peninsula, and had finally pushed forward his holy boundaries to include the mainland of Kilcommon, which completed Erris.

Another name for the barony in the sixteenth century had been Invermore — which was Inbhear mór, the Great Harbour — not only the sea harbour of Blacksod Bay, but a harbour for holy men, a haven for souls.

One of the reasons why Erris had so little history was that it lay at the back of beyond, defended by quagmires. But another reason may have been this particular ecclesiastical tradition. I thought of it as a real sanctuary, in the technical sense, like the churches of the Middle Ages in which even murderers might claim refuge. And in Erris, for that matter, many a murderer had there been.

The actual land of Termoncarragh, where I was now parking the Jaguar in the windy darkness, belonged in the sixteenth century to the Bishopric of Killala. Cattle had been driven there in 1536 'for protection' during one of the local raids or wars. The protection had, as usual, been violated. But this was a land of violence. Why not, thought I, in the commando mood before dawn.

We crouched on the stiff goosebag in the crackling reeds at the edge of the lake, trying to identify its inhabitants by ear. There was a party of white-fronts muttering occasionally. Almost certainly there would be some widgeon, though they were now silent in the darkness. A mallard uttered an interjection once or twice. The wind was away from us, so noises came by gusts. Brownie trembled beside me, more from excitement than cold. She was a rarity — for setters were not supposed to be steady if allowed to retrieve, yet she was fairly good at both. We loved each other more than anything else in the world. The only thing she could not do was to retrieve from water.

Patience is one of the virtues attributed to fishermen and wildfowlers, but of course no patience is necessary. If anything, we were liable to be suffocated by impatience, by the breathless thrill. We tautened in the frozen ambush like assassins, like thugs, like the first and second moorland murderers of Banquo, while Erris, invisible, asserted its lone and ancient personality about us.

Everything in Erris came from the sea, not out from the land. The anseriforms did, which we were there to slaughter, but so had the pirates and the Vikings and the hermits of St Comán. The whole barony was a kind of promontory fort, defended on the landward side from the mainland by its bogs. What little history it had came from the ocean.

For instance, the Armada had passed these stone-fanged cliffs. I knew rather more than most of the locals about this subject, because I had read about it in books, and now, waiting for the sunrise in a bloodthirsty landscape of desolation, bloodthirsty myself, I fell to pondering the story.

In the first Queen Elizabeth's day, the Norman barons who had originally penetrated to the west of Ireland as conquerors had already 'gone native'. The chieftains of Connaught had consisted of the Irish ones like the Donnells or Connors — who claimed descent from goodness knows what races of the Fir Bolg — and the Norman-Irish ones who were descended from William de Burgo. The latter had divided the territory between its two great chiefs, MacWilliam Eighter and MacWilliam Oughter.

Astonishing people! Hooligans is what they are called in America — indeed, there was a Connaught clan called Ó Huallachain. These gangsters, brawlers, Tammany bosses of the dark ages, had passed the time in local wars which were little more

Dawn by the Lake

than gang fights or riots, in assassinations and raids for cattle. Big Terence O'Connor, for instance, whose poetical Irish name was Toirdelbhach Mor O'Conchobhair, had twenty-three sons. His son Rory had blinded his own son Murrough, had been deposed by another son Conor — who was himself murdered — and had died in religion, aged 82. Of Big Terence's first twenty-six descendants through Cathal Crobhderg (Charlie Red-Claw), eleven had died by violence. Of the first nineteen descendants through Muircheantaigh Muimhnaigh, twelve did so. The Bourkes or de Burgos who squabbled with the Connors had been just the same. Their original MacWilliam, Scotty Sir Edmond, had lost five of his first get by the sword. His Elizabethan descendant, the third Richard, had four sons. All four had died suddenly — one of them on the gallows. Another Bourke of this period, Lanky Walter, had eight descendants. Six of them were hanged.

One of the charms of these jokers lay in their nicknames. There was the Blind Abbot, there was Iron Dick, there was the Devil's Hook and the Devil's Hook's Son. Peevish Edmond, Horsy David, Lame Thomas, Swarthy Richard, Learned John, Grey William, Redmond the Whiskers — they would have made up an excellent crew for Long John Silver.

It was among these embattled anarchists that Queen Elizabeth had been trying to extend the royal peace of England by the hand of her Governor, Sir Richard Bingham — when the shattered Armada limped and staggered past, in 1588.

The Spanish soldiers, with their modern arms and military training, were immediately recognized as valuable assets by the mobsters of Mayo, where they were wrecked. Those who had not been massacred by the locals the moment their ship ran ashore were collected by the nearest chieftain — a gentleman probably dressed in serge and pampooties — so that they might be used as fighting slaves. They were unpaid mercenary troops — a melancholy pressed gang. Their alternatives had been to be slain at once on the beaches by the Irish, or to be slain at a later date fighting for the Irish against the English. A certain Sir Murrough O'Flaherty had set great store by a band of about twenty of them, which he had collected.

By December 1588 — that same cold month in which we

were crouching among the reeds of Termoncarragh, but three hundred and fifty years before — twelve ships had been lost upon the coast of Connaught. Two or three had sunk at sea outside the islands. 1,100 men had been put to the sword. 4,600 had been drowned. Don Lewis de Cordova had been collected with his nephew, to await the Queen's orders. The Queen killed Spaniards at once. The chiefs killed them likewise, or conscripted them for future use.

In Tirawley, one ship was taken with four hundred men. Melaughlin Mac an Ab, the son of Angus the Abbot, distinguished himself by slaughtering eighty unarmed castaways with his own Galloglass axe. In Erris itself, there came ashore two vessels. The bewildered, the harried and hopeless southerners were scattered about Broadhaven and Ballycroy. They were trying to band together for self-protection. They were trying to rescue their crews by sea. They were marching hither and thither in pitiful confusion, trying to fortify themselves in primitive castles at Doona and Donamona. A few names have come down to us — Don Alonso de Leyva, who made a stand in Ballycroy, and a certain Giovanni Avancini, who deserted from him with fourteen Italians.

The whole country was up, stirred like an ant's nest. A complicated quarrel about the succession to the MacWilliamship — which Elizabeth had abolished — had been touched off by the arrival of the Armada. England's difficulty had as usual been Ireland's opportunity. Sir Richard Bingham already had his hands full with a different part of the rebellion in Ulster,

and the piratical nicknames of Connaught were forth in strength
— some killing the dons, some enrolling them against the Queen,
some conspiring against one another. The sons of the Blind
Abbot were out, with those of Iron Dick and Lanky Walter and
the Devil's Hook's Son. Mac an Demain an Chorain was his
name, literally the Son of the Demon of the Reaping Hook.
His hook or sickle may possibly have been a clan talisman
or tribal fetish, like the pruning knife of the O'Connells in
Kerry.

The troubles continued until the peace of 1589 — complicated,
gory and barbarous. Bingham caught a certain Justin MacDon-
nell, tried him by martial law for having helped to bring Don
Alonso inland, and hanged him there and then. A loyal
Mr Browne was ambushed and slain by the Son of the Demon.
Sir Murrough O'Flaherty's son, having been captured, was held
as a hostage. But Sir Murrough's fellow rebels offered him £300
to raise a bodyguard, £300 to break down the castle of Augh-
nanure, and £300, in compensation, if his hostage son was
hanged. These terms proving acceptable to Sir Murrough, he
took the £900, did break down the castle, and his son *was*
hanged — at a profit of £300 to himself. Everybody thought
the arrangement reasonable — everybody, perhaps, except his
twenty Spanish mercenaries, 'who', it is said, 'could not endure
the hardships of Irish life.'

A Lieutenant Francis Bingham slew a hundred at castle
Annacare on March 30th, executing most of the wounded and
prisoners, and 'there was gotten of their furniture 63 pieces,

besides other furnitures, as morions, swords, sculls and targets, and four guidons.'

Sir Richard Bingham, who finally dealt with the rebellion with skill and energy, like most colonial administrators, was hampered and betrayed by the intrigues of his own government. Appeasement of the rebels, dictated to him from home, was assumed by the enemy to be a sign of weakness. It was not until 1589 that the rising was brought to a submission. Then the third clause of the treaty, signed by seven Englishmen with their names and by ten Irishmen with their marks — for they were all illiterate, including Sir Murrough and the Blind Abbot — stated that they, the Irish, should 'forthwith deliver to the Lord Deputy such Spaniards, Portagalls, and other foreignors of the Spanish fleet as are now amongst them.'

Thinking of those unlucky dagoes, as we crouched by the lakeside which had refused them sanctuary or compassion, I began to think too about the taking of life. I never minded much about the killing of humans — provided they were adult, male and other than myself. After all, Homo Sapiens was the most successful and most terrible of the raptors — far more terrifying and destructive than the wolves and tigers which almost always fled at the sight of him. He was the only animal from which everything else ran away. Foxes could walk by river banks without frightening fish, and fish could swim without scaring the passing birds. When man passed, there was a hush in every element. Also, out of about half a million species, he was one of the only eight kinds I could think of that indulged in warfare. Six of the eight were ants. True warfare meant joining together in bands to fight against bands of the same species — it was not war if a band of wolves attacked a band of sheep — and, out of all those hundreds of thousands, only man and a few insects did it. In the animal world, warfare was a much rarer vice than incest or cannibalism or the everyday simplicity of murder.

Very well, if man was that kind of creature, he could hardly complain when he sometimes got butchered himself. He was able to look after his own life. He was self-competent. Wisely enough, he seldom trusted his fellow men.

It seemed to me that the unpardonable kind of killing was when you killed something which was not self-competent and which did trust you. Women or children or horses or dogs or even domestic cattle, which reposed their faith in the protection of man: it did seem, even when I was a shooter, that there was something monstrous in betraying their confidence. It was an outrage on the dignity of the beast to refuse mercy, after the wonderful compliment of being expected to give it.

So what about those Spaniards, whose gaunt forgotten ghosts now wheeled about us in the winter wind? They had hardly been competent, poor shipwrecked sods, and perhaps, like all castaways who have survived the forces of nature, they did hope for compassion from their fellow men. Or perhaps they did not expect it? Perhaps, in the days of Elizabeth the First, they only expected to be 'put to the sword'. It was a condition of warfare then, by no means confined to Ireland.

'Put to the sword.' Why was this phrase active, as it were, instead of passive? Surely the sword was put to them? And yet there was a horrible vividness about it — the shrinking flesh thrust forward struggling to the point which pierced it.

And what about the wild geese of Termoncarragh? Most habitual shooters console themselves for the massacres they perpetrate by a series of clichés. Sometimes they claim that they only 'shoot for the pot', i.e. that everything killed by them is for the useful and necessary purpose of being eaten. Others seem to be compensated by the remark that 'a man must kill the thing he loves.' I myself used to claim that it was so difficult to achieve a goose that the achievement was itself beautiful, more beautiful than the living goose — a piece of casuistry which does not consider the feelings of the victim.

Geese like rats, are among the most intelligent and affectionate of animals, and they seem to have a moral sense. There is a true goose story in W. H. Hudson, which is always worth repeating. It concerns an island off the coast of Norway, whose farmer's poultry suffered from a plague of foxes. He had to collect the fowls at night to lock them up, and he set a fox trap against his adversary. Instead of a fox, this trap caught a wild goose on migration, breaking its leg. It was an elderly white-front — evidently, by the massive bars on its breast, a patriarch and leader of the squadron. The farmer took it home, made a splint for the leg, and released it with clipped wings among his domestic birds. Some time later, after it had recovered, he began to notice on his evening rounds that the fowls were already collected in the chicken house when he went to lock them up. Watching to discover the reason, he found that that old admiral — that captive marshal of the air —had assumed the leadership of his fellow prisoners. By his own intelligence, watching the farmer, he had understood the process of the nightly lock-up, and now he himself was collecting the chickens at the right time, to parade them for bed.

There is another story in Hudson about a man who shot a teal, breaking its wing. For some reason, he took it home and made a pet of it, though it could no longer fly. It forgave the injury and became devoted to him. He was a business man, and it used to meet him every evening at the end of the street, on foot, as he came home from work.

Such were the creatures for whom Brownie and I laid wait before dawn that morning, fingering a B.S.A. magnum charged with BB shot. It was right for Brownie: it was her nature. But I was begining to wonder if it was right for me.

A red line like a streak of blood between the black, horizontal, menacing clouds, tattered at their tops, showed that it was time for sunrise. Out at sea, beyond the sandy graveyard of Termoncarragh where the white clay pipes lay in cardboard boxes among the coffins, the leaning wind was slicing the tips from the waves in a haze which was half sea, half air. On the low, sheep-nibbled down of Annagh, which was beginning to loom into a grey daylight, stood the abandoned home of Bingham Lodge — named after those same Binghams, now Earls of Lucan, who had fought the Armada and later charged at Balaclava. The sleepy farmer of the inland hillside, in his white cottage with the black turf-stacks, lay still abed.

On the choppy lake and around it, there began to be a coming and going, like the stir of an early market. A party of widgeon, whistling whee-oo, whee-oo, careered along the stream of air, out of range. White-fronts, well aware of the human presence, hoved at the further margins, or, taking a trip, toured the middle air beyond gunshot. A thrilling consort of swans, whom I had not seen there before, came beating in against the gale. They were not mute swans, but smaller ones, either Bewicks or Whoopers, whose cry was a smothered sort of yapping. Probably they were Bewicks. The bending reeds combed the wind's hair, the thin ice crackled or grated, and Brownie trembled, trembled, her eyes fixed on the sky.

A single swan, not a Bewick or Whooper, came head-on towards us, labouring against the element, hardly fifteen feet above the water. With black nares and frowning eye, her great wings twanging and the long neck sighted on her destination, she made her way along the lake, well within range. The noise of her wings was plangent and regular like somebody hammering with a pliable hammer, or like the measured swishing of some terrible cane, but metallic and melodious too, like a Hawaiian guitar or a musical saw.

Ever since I had learned to fly an aeroplane I had wondered, for this was before the second world war, what it would be like to shoot down a Heinkel. That swan, that vast and snowy wingspread, was a bomber, not a bird.

I stood up when she was abreast of us, slipping the safety-catch, and hesitated with the gun half raised.

There was a superstition in Ireland, probably connected with the legendary children of Lir — who were supposed to have been turned into swans — that it was unlucky to shoot these creatures. In England, it was illegal. Besides, what was the use of shooting swans? Although they had been eaten in the Middle Ages, it was doubtful whether anybody would know how to cook them now. Also, even at that moment, I dimly perceived that beauty did not only exist to be destroyed.

However, the temptation was too strong. I had never shot a swan. All shooters are really trying to prove their doubted manhood, the gun being their virility. I did not want to go home unfulfilled. I did want to find out about the Heinkels. In my mind's eye, I could imagine the great neck hurtling down head foremost into a cloud of spray.

When I shot the swan, she did not make a nose dive. It dawned on me, while she was still in the air, that her centre of gravity must be astern, not ahead. She paused in the wind, all aback, surprised, hanging on the stall with the ailerons of her secondary feathers going soggy — then slid down backwards, on an ungainly tail-slip, into the water.

The gale, blowing away from us, carried the useless corpse further and further from the shore.

Brownie, no water-dog, stood beside me watching it, as the choppy wavelets dandled it out of reach. Two or three white feathers danced beside the soggy hulk, curled into dainty cusps like wood shavings. What had once been beautiful was as dead as a dago — and as pointlessly.

WE started from the little villag at six o'clock in the mornin passing through Westport about nine. We drove th Jaguar into a two-shilling en closure and climbed out, th four of us, leaving poor Brownie inside. It was felt that it woul not be respectful to take a dog to the holy mountain, on th 28th of July. The Catholic dogma was that animals have n

souls. Peasants in the west, on entering a house, would sometimes say with exactness: 'God save all here, barring the dog and
the cat.' Well, at least they recognized the presence of domestic
animals in the home — which English peasants on a similar visit
might not be polite enough to notice, perhaps.

There was Jack, gentle, friendly, smiling and optimistic,
stating that he was 'as happy as Larry'. There was Mrs O'Callaghan, fervent, loving, tall, thin, humble and frequently
exclaiming that everything was 'loverlay'. It was a tremendous
day for her who lived half her life in simple dreams of holiness
and miracles and soothsayers. There was her stout sister Mrs
Reilly, the grocer's wife, humorous, bold, selfish, prolific, good
company — a joky woman who was able to look after herself in
any circumstances. And I was there, the driver, beginning to
blink awake. We wore stout shoes or boots and carried black-
thorn walking-sticks.

The two east-coast women, whom I had fetched the previous
day from Kildare on an old promise, looked at the great Croagh
with interest and complacency. They had no standards in their
minds by which to judge mountains. Even looking at it, they
had no idea what they were in for. A blanched statue of St Patrick
was before them, past which the endless trail of pilgrims wound
up the slope like ants. Two thousand five hundred and ten feet
they ascended — the last part up a cone shaped like a pyramid,
and nearly as steep as one. On the top, a minute cube, was the
saint's chapel, on the saint's own alp, named after him, and this
was the day when Ireland went to visit him. It nearly always

misted or poured with rain on the 28th, but our visit was to be blessed unusually. The weather was superb.

Jack and I, accustomed to long days on the heather in pursuit of grouse or wildfowl, found it difficult to keep back with the ladies. We waited for them twice, dawdled, went back for them — but the third time Jack said with a shake of his head, 'They will never do it.' The last mass on top was at noon, and he wanted to be there in time. We returned along the line of climbers to the toiling women, already after a few hundred feet practically foundered, and broke the news. We were going on, to be in time for mass, and the females were to take it easy. They were to rest often, and to give in, if forced, at the first Station. In their Dublin clothes, but fortunately with low heels, they waved the menfolk on. They were speechless. Mrs O'Callaghan, as thin as a rake from doing Lough Deag the previous week, was a buttered parsnip in the growing heat of the morning. The sweat stood out on each side of her nose. She was white at her cheek bones. We knew she had a weak heart, and felt frightened. But she, no believer in dying for a good cause, knew that the good cause would preserve her from dying. She was indomitable. Her hat was crooked.

Mrs Reilly, a mountain climbing a mountain, stumped in her wake, fifty yards behind, weeping and sweating in black satin. She had already fallen down twice and cut her knee, but she forged ahead with an expression of martyrdom — with plaintive, ceaseless petitions to God, or to Mrs O'Callaghan, or to all and sundry. She was full of courage too, inside her balloon of a bosom, although imploring with every other breath to be allowed to sit down. 'Oh, holy mother of God, does it be much furder?' We had hardly begun. Her tall, staunch sister, refusing to waste breath on words, merely shook the crooked hat. Excelsior. We left them to it.

The first two thousand feet were easy, like any other mountain. We took them flippantly, relishing and marking our fellow pilgrims, into whose line we had become absorbed. They scrambled up, five or six yards apart, in ones and twos and threes, while a thinner line of returning visitors swung freely down, accomplished, hallowed, pleased with themselves or amused at us climbers.

It dawned on me that we were back in the Canterbury Tales. No wonder Chaucer was good-humoured. For the mountainside was in a state of fellowship — it was happy, bonhommous, mutually congratulating. Although the population of Eire was counted in millions, people kept meeting others whom they knew. And when they met, they stopped. They encountered with a great handshake. They teased and joked and laughed, far from holy or hushed. They were the very characters out of Chaucer, vulgar and surprising. There was the Wif of Bath, closely resembling Mrs Reilly, but now black in the face with agony and determination. And there, coming down, was an acquaintance from our own village, Inspector Ryan, saluting us with welcome. Six elderly peasants from Shrataggle, friends of ours and famous for having won some money in the Irish Sweepstake, were tramping gaily past. The eldest, the actual holder of the winning ticket, shook my hand with compliment, averring that after this we should doubtless meet in heaven. He qualified it by adding that — at least — one of us might get there. This was a beautiful tease. He had said it as if he meant that I was the good one, he the reprobate. Yet he knew quite well that I was a Protestant, and thus he could leave me, in high good-humour and a slight aura of whisky, to puzzle it out. Then there was the bookie from Belfast! There was no slightness about his aura. It rose from him in a visible mist, which would have exploded in a blue flame if he had struck a match. He was wearing a thick winter overcoat, which he had forgotten — and this was the sunniest pilgrimage in the forty-odd years since the chapel had been built. He reeled from side to side of the break-neck path, singing and exhorting himself. His scarlet face was covered with carbuncles. He had been drinking whisky in the train since midnight. When we asked him whether he thought he would get there safely, he replied: 'I'm from Belfast, I am. Och aye!' Next there was the old, old lady going down. She was past eighty, and could not put one foot in front of the other. She could advance a foot, and draw the other up to it, but that was all she could do. Or was this perhaps for a vow? She had started at one o'clock the previous night, heard mass at dawn, and would be home at about ten. There she went softly and surely, foot up to foot, carrying her eighty years patiently down a gradient of one in four — such a morsel of light old bones that she strayed and drifted like thistledown. There was also the photographer from Dublin, a young fellow of thirty or so, but a city man with feet as tender as your face. He had been on the pilgrimage fourteen times, and loved the mountain. This time, he had decided to go barefoot. We stopped beside him for breath, and noticed that the naked foot which he was putting down on the sharp flints was trembling from the pain. It shook in an ague of agony, as he, at a snail's pace, moved on in torment.

The last five hundred feet were the worst. The tireless Jack, always as fit as a flea, led up like a will o' the wisp, while I dragged my clumsier body over the torrent of flint which had to be taken on hands and knees. Jack said, 'Don't look up. If you look, you will lose heart.' The pilgrims, slithering down, seemed likely to sweep us back to the foot.

I began to pray.

People *in extremis*, even agnostics we are told, generally do pray — but I was not so far gone as that. I had not come on the pilgrimage for exalted motives. I enjoyed mountains, I wanted to see what the festival was like, and, in a moment of aberration, I had once mentioned to Mrs O'Callaghan that one day I would take her. The beatific expression on her face, when she heard this promise, had seemed impossible to disappoint.

But I was praying all the same. It was partly like the curses uttered by men in desperate struggles, and partly, I am ashamed to say, it was to impress Jack. I moved my lips so that he could see. On the other hand, less ignoble, how could one not pray when everybody else was doing so? Surely it is better to be with people than against them, and would it not have been churlish to resist the hospitality of faith which surrounded us?

At last there was the blessed top — all 2,500 feet of it — with the tiny, weather-worn chapel on its small table-land, and the whole world at prayer also in the sunlight above Clew Bay.

We parted and began to make our circuits of the chapel separately. We were supposed to go round seven times, saying the rosary. Five hundred people were doing the same thing, in a whirligig of worship, people of every age, in every kind of suit, lost in their own errands of petition or atonement.

It must have been the altitude which made me pray, or the glorious weather, or the superabundant feeling of health and happiness which comes after exertion, or the vastness of the view, or the common unconsciousness in which my miniature ego was now submerged. At all events I sauntered along with a rosary, presenting my soul and all others to the God in whom I did not believe at sea level.

The point was that it was not possible in that bright air to pray for yourself or for other individuals: not even for Mrs O'Callaghan, who was always praying for me. It was hardly possible to pray for the human race even — for its peace or forgiveness or anything like that — because it seemed wrong to pray for anything. You could hold it out to its maker — like a man who has been run over, mutely displaying his maimed stumps. As we moved round and round so strangely, with the three hundred and sixty-five islands of the bay like toys at our feet, and Clare island a peep-show and the White Cow island beyond — with Corslieve fifty miles to the north, and Achill hinting a shoulder, and the universal sea about, it was only possible to hold out the tragic filth of the human race for God to see — not feeling contempt for them, nor expecting anything to be done for them — without petition or sarcasm or confusion of mind.

I thought how the world had never been at peace. Even when Europe was not at war, China would be fighting. If China had peace, the strife would move to South America or somewhere else. Such was the human species that the whole globe had probably never been bloodless since men invented agriculture. And here we were, members of it along with the other members, revolving the top of a holy hill and not knowing what to ask. It was possible to think of the unfathomable wickedness of man, his carnivorous ferocity. It was possible to think of the other beasts, rooks and ants and mackerel and bees and wolves, five hundred thousand species perhaps, among whom there were only about eight kinds who indulged in warfare like man. It was not possible to feel superior or bitter to one's fellows about it, for we were all in the same boat. But, in the high sunshine, it did seem within the bounds of possibility that we who were there walking, now innocently occupied for the few moments of this pilgrimage, might humbly and not despairingly regard ourselves as presentable. Presentable. There was nothing we could ask. But now, for this moment in the year, those of us who had got there could presume to draw attention to our condition. At any other time, it would be wiser to hide. But there, today, together, perhaps men could say: Look. Look at the pickle we are in, please God.

So I tramped round, telling the beads and presenting my species to the infinity which surrounded us, and which also governed the half-moon, just visible in daylight, hanging part way up the dazzling blue over remote Nephin.

I noticed from the tail of my eye that the Archbishop of Tuam was darting round a circle near the chapel, offering his ring to be kissed.

We had known that he would be there. Half-way up the mountain, we had heard the rumour. 'The Archbishop is on the top!' It was scarcely nine-thirty when we heard it, and he had reached the top at scarcely nine-thirty, yet the whole concourse had known at once, with exultation. The Reek had transfigured itself by knowing that its archbishop was at the focus as their captain, and everybody had told everybody else.

A circle of serge and fishermen's jerseys was jostling inward to kiss the ring of Tuam, rather as a rugby-football scrum presses in, but on their knees, and the good man at the centre, rapidly flirting his hand hither and thither above the bowed heads, bestowed it among them.

I gave up my circumambulation to join the throng. I was exalted with the pilgrimage and I wanted to kiss the ring — without reservations or double meanings and not from curiosity and not so that I could say that I had done so and not, oddly enough, because I had any belief in it as a source of blessing. But it was a source of virtue and affection. It was right, at this altitude of common union with the species, to do what was being done. In Ireland, on that particular day, feeling at one with the race, it was good, right, proper and your bounden duty to accept the symbol of unity. I dumped myself down on the outskirts of the scrum and began to shuffle forward on aching knees.

The Archbishop had to offer the ring — an insanitary practice, the faithless might sourly think — to several thousand people. The newspapers, hopelessly exaggerating as ever, said that there were forty thousand on the peak. There could not have been less than fifteen thousand during the day. An Archbishop, in these circumstances, could hardly be interested in individuals or in particular blessings. All he could do was to press the ring to one mouth after another, at the same time rapidly muttering such general good wishes as he could muster in benediction. Round went the hard and not very expensive jewel: the words, sharing themselves among so many, were a hasty but warmly intended jabber. He was blessing them racially, not as units, and his strength was taxed.

When I got there, I kissed like the others. My heart suddenly overflowed for all the people in the world, and I bussed it like a lover. It was not a peck on the cheek, but a good hug — on the mouth, as it were.

For a fraction of a second the startled old clergyman, who must have been feeling giddy as he revolved, saw an individual in sharp focus. He said to me personally, 'God bless you,' as if from his heart.

Numbed by this electric contact. I hoisted myself from my

knees to resume the circles round the chapel. I stumbled off over the loose stones, warning myself not to exaggerate and to realize that the private moment must have been an illusion.

After another turn, a bright and perky young chaplain, walking widdershins against the revolutions which the crowd was making, caught me and fished me out. 'Who are you, and what is your profession? His Grace would like to talk to you.'

The situation had ceased to be real. The merry chaplain had called the Archbishop 'His Grace', so I knew that this was the right thing to call him. I told the chaplain awkwardly that I would come whenever I was told to, but that surely His Grace would be too busy? I was overcome with shame inside myself, for not being a Catholic, for being where I had no business to be, for being a kind of Judas, loved in treachery. I lied to the chaplain, saying that I was a convert. It was a strange lie. It was not to save myself from humiliation, but to save the Archbishop. It seemed impossible to disappoint *him*.

The chaplain told me to present myself at any time. He said that His Grace would be there till afternoon. He minced away.

I did not, did not, did not want to meet the prelate. I did not want to be found out as a foreigner and a humbug, to be cast out from the communion. I did not want to let the old man down after our flash. I knew that I must not deceive him.

I put the tangle aside and went to look for Mrs O'Callaghan.

Each time that we had made a circuit, I had spent a few

minutes looking down the last, precipitous incline, in case the two dauntless female escalators of our party might have made good. This time, I found Mrs O'Callaghan at the second station, white-faced, perspiring, pallid, unbeatable. I made her get up from her knees, insisting that she must walk gently round the chapel once or twice to cool off, before she kneeled again in the high breeze. She was reluctant to do this. So I tied up her scarf, lent her my mackintosh, and left her to her own devices. Before I went, I could not resist telling her gruffly, like a small boy boasting of a cricketer's autograph, that I had been sent for by the Archbishop. Mrs O'Callaghan's heart missed a beat. She had always known that Mr White was a saint!

When I had finished my rounds, I kneeled on the cruel stones in front of the chapel where they were saying mass, and beat my breast.

There was a confused time while I wondered what to do. I ran into the bookie from Belfast, now safely at the top and stone-cold sober. I smiled at Jack in the passing whirligig. Mrs Reilly in black satin, still alive, limping as she cooled, carried her portly bosom affably by. I talked to the unshod photographer, with his ugly, bony, ivory, trembling feet. I was shirking the rendezvous.

The next thing was a sermon by another bishop. He was a tub of lard whom you could willingly have pushed over a cliff. In his mauve hat and scarlet facings he stood on a table, like a pig's face cooked by a first-class chef and powdered with flour — with the sour lemon of his sermon in his mouth — and there he preached away with three stock gestures his loveless, nationalistic, anti-British, political oratory about Ireland and St Patrick. His facts about the patron saint — whichever three people the latter may have been — were misrepresented. His consciousness of humanity and of love and of the griefs of the wide world was *nil*. His slightly menacing conclusion seemed to be that the ambition of Jesus Christ was to be an Irishman and a castrato.

Tired by this plump, proud, futile and scholiastic porker, I looked round the lovely faces which were listening to him in simple faith — and there, suddenly, I saw that we were not alone. Wheeling round the apex of the reek, while the fat man babbled with his three play-actor's movements, there was a pair of ravens. Not crows, ravens. In the midst there was the purple man. Round him there were the dumb humans, at their best. And round them, wheeling in the free air of Padraig's mountain, were the two exquisite, interested birds — coal-black, primaries bending, septuagenarian, monogamous, at home.

A priest, standing behind me during the sermon, had decided that my strange beard and questing nose would make a good subject for a photograph. Others began to photograph me. I stood patiently for them, bashful, at a loss, like a sheep, for several pictures. Interrogated, I repeated the lie about being a convert. I repeated it emphatically, for a hideous suspicion had begun to grow in my mind.

Could they — was it possible — could they suspect that I was St Patrick?

We were in the atmosphere of miracles at that altitude, and country people do believe in miracles. There was the beard. There was the — well, you could almost say holiness, certainly a kind of elevation, with which I had lately been behaving — and the Archbishop had sent for me. Everybody in Ireland notices everything at once. Every sidelong glance, I now realized, must have seen the kiss, the chaplain. Every subtle ear on the grape-vine must have known of the message. I blundered off in an agony of shame — to find myself eye to eye with Tuam.

God, let him not think so too!

He asked: 'Did you come up fasting?'

'Yes.' It was not true. I had drunk some tea and eaten bread-and-butter at half-past five, but truth and falsehood were confused. I only felt that I must tell him what he wanted to be told.

It was an Irish trait. The sacred mountain had quite transmogrified the Englishman.

'Then you must come with me and have a cup of tea.'

The cameras clicked on us as we were ushered into the chapel. The worshippers, crowded against the altar rail, made way for us, all eyes, as we shoved our way past the rail, past where benediction was going on — to the minute vestry behind it. They were waiting for the miracle.

The vestry, already overcrowded by three women and several priests standing, was occupied by the pork-bishop, eating the leg of a cold chicken at a table which just had room for three.

A nice cup of tea on the summit

'Who is this fellow?' he asked his chaplain — more worldly and less spiritual than Tuam. He glanced at me with hostile, patriotic eye-slit, scarcely saluting his superior. A practical politician, living acutely in his realistic arrangement of facts, he knew the visitor at once for an alien and a spy. His thoughts were as plain as if they had been written on his forehead: 'What on earth has the old fool got hold of now?' He gobbled in silence, in silence packed up his traps, and shortly afterwards departed with his chaplain, after a terse goodbye, not looking or speaking to the infidel. I miserably mumbled a chicken wing and sucked cool tea in the third seat at this distinguished table.

But the Archbishop was not an old fool. Now that there was a pause in the march of events, and in the picnic vestry less action over the passing of plates, it was possible to examine him covertly. He was a small man of about seventy, with a pronounced chin and nose, wedge-shaped, almost like Mr Punch's, compact of character. I remembered that there was a carved figure of a bishop on a small pillar at Killadera, Fermanagh, which resembled him minutely. There was a slight blemish on the bridge of his nose. In spite of his evident charity, and indeed his sanctity, the nose and chin were not the ones to stand any nonsense. He was hospitable, simple, pleased, direct, keen, receptive, unselfconscious, interested in people: but he treated his guest as an Archbishop should, familiarly, by no means vulgarly. It was a penetrating eye, if a warm one, which sparkled behind the great nose, well able to rebuke sin firmly with silence, by being sorry about it.

I was over-awed, charmed, flattered and wretched. The worshippers could partly see us through the altar door, which I hated, and now there was this about having to confess that I was not a convert. I had been instructed as a Catholic, but had rejected the faith at the last moment. My delicacy or honour or whatever it ought to be called was wound in a knot.

It was like this. If a man falls in love with a woman who actually dislikes him, she does not tell him so, but temporizes in an awkward way, not wishing to hurt his feelings. In the same way, the crestfallen excursionist (me) who had set foot upon Croagh Patrick as if on a Cook's Tour, could not now bring himself to hurt a trusting friend, by telling him that he was an agnostic. It was not shame. It was the Archbishop that I was protecting.

To my astonishment, I was spared all explanation. With the exit of the purple man, an air of gaiety — positively of levity and disrespect — came over the little vestry. The Archbishop said teasingly to his perky chaplain, pretending to bully him, 'Of course, you haven't done this pilgrimage at all. Look at all those people going round and doing their stations.' The chaplain calmly replied, unless my shocked ears deceived me: 'My dear sir, I carried up that *bag*!' And he pointed to the vestments. While the priests at the altar on the other side of the partition blessed beads and the people kneeling at the rails peered through the door, His Grace talked cheerfully about Oberammergau, where he had been on this day last year — about one of the women handing round the chicken, who, like Mrs O'Callaghan, had only come out of Loch Deag on Friday — about myself and the village I came from and the West of Ireland and what I did in it, for he was an interested Grace, willing to be informed about everything — about his own main trouble in getting up the mountain — which had been, being impeded by having to bless people. He asked more than he talked. I told him with a loving heart how he must always come up the Reek, every year, because the whole mountain had known of his presence the moment he was there, and I told him what pleasure he had given. It was agreed that he would come. Then I told about the naomhóg of Inniskea, and got permission to fish it out of the sea if I could. At last the spry, noble old shepherd began to drift towards the door. I kneeled to be blessed, and was surprised to hear the natural, conversational voice, coming from over my head afterwards, inviting me for a visit at his palace in Tuam.

There were some booths on the summit, where it was possible to buy sixpenny lemonade at half a crown a bottle or sausage rolls or tea at a shilling a cup. Received back into the real world with silent awe by my friends, I sat with Jack and Mrs O'Callaghan and Mrs Reilly on a pile of stones, radiating sanctity and consuming tea. They were all dewy with fulfilment, like the freshness of the earth after a thunderstorm and rain. The people of the pilgrimage, now more or less over, paraded about, laughed, joked, codded and haggled at the booths. ('Half a dollar for a bottle of lemonade!' 'Let ye carry up a bottle yerself, ma'am, and I'll slip ye three shillings for it.') We pulled ourselves together reluctantly, to leave the superb view and our spiritual pleasure, for the happy journey down the mountainside to find poor Brownie baking in the car.

In the public house on level ground, where women were not welcome, Jack and I had two drinks, and took two out to our friends. The interior was full of drunk men, celebrating their happiness on the hill. They had been drunk with God up there, and now, by a perfectly natural transition, they were carrying on with porter down here. Nothing could have been more reasonable and simple than this. They were hardy and thirsty from their exertions, which made them hanker for the gullet-swelling gulp of stout, and they were also, for these few moments, as innocent as Adam before the fall. Their sins had been left on the summit when they went to the altar, so there was plenty of room for new ones. Also, they had loved each other on high, and they wanted to prolong the comradeship, with loving cups.

One man, with a voice of velvet, sang 'The Rose of Tralee' so that it would make a chasm of the heart. Another, an accomplished *diseur*, related a ghost story with the mastery of an artist, to the whole bar, silent as mice.

It was about a rich farmer who had a haunted room, and anybody who slept in it was dead by the morning. He offered his daughter's hand in marriage to any person who could survive the night. So poor Paddy, the conquering under-dog of all Irish folklore, said that he would be able for the adventure. When midnight came, a sepulchral voice sang through the roof: 'I'm falling! I'm falling!' 'Fall away then,' said Paddy. Whereat, down came a pair of boots: into them fell a pair of legs: on to the legs dropped a body: a head tumbled down and clapped on top. Two others came like that (the ghost's father and grandfather) and all were dressed in leggings and three-cornered hats. At last down came a football, and they began to play. Paddy joined the game to make an even number, and there they played all night until the sweat ran down his back. Towards cockcrow he plucked up courage to address their honours, asked if he could do anything for them, and was told that by this question he had saved his life. It turned out that these ghosts had been misers and debt-defaulters during their lifetime, and he was to pull out an indicated secret drawer. With the money and the old debt-accounts in it, he was to make restitution for the wrongs they had done. At that they vanished, and when the surprised farmer came to Paddy, he found the room as empty as a burner (saucepan) turned upside down. Restitution was made, and Paddy married the daughter.

This good story was told according to a mode, obviously in an invariable word-form. although the narrator was tipsy.

Back in our home village, at seven or eight o'clock that evening, the pilgrims had great welcome. People seemed anxious to have contact, i.e. in conversation, with us, as though we brought back a goodness which they could share. Jack's wife had cooked us a banquet, after which there was a sing-song and many stories. We went to bed at midnight, replenished with our happy day. I was determined to regularize my spiritual relations with the Archbishop, by being baptized as soon as possible. Of course I never was.

Just as I went to sleep, I remembered an incident on the return journey, at the foot of the Reek. They were asking money there, for the expenses of the chapel. After I had given some silently, they had thanked me. 'Thank you very much indeed, sir.' When I was still silent, they tried again. 'Go raibh mile maith agat.'

But I had only bowed. I had not wanted them there, at that time, to hate my English accent.

I F you write about Irishmen as if they were clowns, like those Irish R.M. books, they resent it. We want to be taken seriously.'

'I should be more likely to write about you as if you were villains.'

'Well, that's better than being a clown, anyway. But it is not rue.'

'What is true?'

'Ah, Jaysus,' he said, putting on the accent, 'sure, isn't

everybody in Eire explaining what we are to everybody else? And all the explanations are different.'

He smiled from the chair on the opposite side of the turf fire, an enormous hulk of manhood. I am not a small man myself, being well over six feet, but he could have cracked me in one hand like a walnut. He was one of the few Gaels who never blamed people for being English. He was open-minded and well-read and as friendly as he was huge. He was as intelligent as he was friendly.

'In the West,' he said, 'we are simple.'

'Simple, my foot! You are so damned subtle — you see round so many corners — that you spend half the time gazing up your own backsides.'

'That's true too.'

'They can't both be true.'

'Why not?'

He thought hard and added slowly: 'By simple, I mean that we respond to facts, not theories.'

'Like women do?'

'Or children.'

'All children are savages.'

'I never said we were not savages. If you include women and children, I am glad to be a savage. In the West we are innocent.'

'Innocent! Good God! You spend the other half of your time shooting the landlords from behind hedges.'

'Ach, that's an innocent occupation anyway. Besides, we nearly always miss. Did I tell ye the time we shot the parish priest? They were driving home together in his lordship's pony-trap after dark ...'

'Now you are giving me the Irish R.M. stuff yourself, Seán.'

He paused.

'Well,' he said eventually, 'we *are* innocent and we *are* simple. With innocent simplicity we respond directly to facts — which are often complex and subtle. Don't you see how much more difficult it is to go on responding sensitively to fresh facts, rather than to live by rule of thumb like the English? Englishmen are lazy and dull. They make themselves ten commandments or regulations which you could write out on a sixpenny bit, and then they stolidly live by them. Irishmen and all women and children, yes, and savages too, tend to live practically, alertly, according to the delicate situation — not according to ten theories. We are spontaneous. It is far more difficult.'

'Seán, you and your Land Commission — you are a sort of landlord yourself now. Don't they shoot at you nowadays?'

He put his hand in his pocket and threw me a letter two days old.

'I have an album full,' he said.

It was an incoherent, anonymous, threatening scrawl, beginning, 'We are eigh tennants Ballybawneen ...' and ending with 'so watch yourself.' I read it with dismay.

'What are you going to do about it?'

'Put it in the album.'

'Oughtn't you to tell the police — the guards?'

He was delighted.

'What for?'

'Well …'

'I have to go to Ballybawneen next week at all events and I'll find out what it's all about. Come too, if you like. There's a wee lake in the bog there which is supposed to have great trout in it, and you could fish while I am doing the business.'

'I should like to.'

'They don't mean any harm.'

I read it again with revulsion, like suddenly finding an adder on one's path.

'May I keep this letter? Could you spare it? To stick in my diary?'

'Why not? We have plenty more.'

'Seán, it's all very well being spontaneous and so on, but sometimes it revolts me. It is so … so untidy. You never know where you are.'

'All the more interesting to be there.'

'Look,' I said. 'I wouldn't say this to anybody except you, so don't be cross with me. But sometimes the Irish stick in my gullet. I suppose I stick in theirs. It is difficult for different races to get on with each other.'

'It is like being married. It needs forbearance on both sides.'

'But all this whining about the English. All this rot about English tyranny and the holy, innocent Irish that butter wouldn't melt in the mouth of. All this falsification of history. Do you know that the ignorant bigot De Valera has publicly stated how he bases his interest in history on the works of A. M. Sullivan?'

'And who was Sullivan, may I ask?'

'I can tell you who he was not. He was so well educated that he was not even a Bachelor of Arts.'

'Education is not everything.'

'Look, Seán. History is an important thing. It is serious — like science. Emotion is a bad guide to it. You have to know the facts, and be true to them — dispassionately. Do you know about Laudabiliter?'

'Is that the bull by which some Pope or other gave Ireland to the English?'

'Yes, and Sullivan's story about how it happened makes me so angry that I can remember several bits of it by heart. May I recite them to you?'

'Go ahead.'

'He says that Henry the Second wanted to add Ireland "to his English crown" and "an Englishman, Pope Adrian, now sat in the chair of St Peter". "The cunning and politic Henry saw his opportunity" and applied to the holy father for permission to invade the island. Then we get: "Pope Adrian is said to have complied by issuing a bull approving of Henry's scheme ... There is no such bull now to be found in the Papal archives, yet it is credited that some such bull was issued; but its contents, terms and permissions have been absurdly misrepresented and exaggerated." Am I boring you?'

'Not a bit.'

'Well now, will you look at this tissue of false hints? In the first place, there were *no* Englishmen at the time of Laudabiliter.

The *Normans* had conquered the *Saxons* in a frightful pogrom only ninety years before, and the two races hated each other. Henry was a Norman who talked French and the Pope was a Saxon who did not talk what we call English. If there was one man in the world who ought *not* to have wanted to help King Henry, it was Adrian. So much for the "English" king who got Ireland from an "English" pope.'

'You surprise me.'

'And now about "is said" to have been issued, and "no such bull to be found in the Papal archives". The reason why it is not to be found in the archives is that very few of the bulls of the twelfth century *are* to be found there anyway. They have paid the price of age and vanished in the course of eight hundred years. *But*, Seán — *but* — we do have a contemporary version given by Giraldus Cambrensis — a Welshman — and in any case *the next Pope, Alexander III, renewed the grant of Ireland to England in 1172 and his letters on the subject do exist*! Why did the learned Mr Sullivan leave all this out?'

'Dear me!'

'What's more,' said I in triumph, 'another Pope, John XXII, repeated the terms of Laudabiliter to Edward II in 1317. Does this look like "is said" to have been issued?'

'The point being,' explained Seán cheerfully, 'that it is difficult for the Catholic Irish to make out a logical case against the heretic English, without being rude to the Catholic Pope.'

'I'll say it's difficult.'

'But I have just been explaining to you that we are not logical.'

'Then why do you argue at all? You can't argue without being logical.'

'Doesn't everybody argue? Don't women argue? It seems to me that you are in the position of trying to explain something to a wife. You may as well give it up.'

'Women ...'

'Look, Tim,' he said, throwing me a cigarette, 'are you putting this forward as an argument for England governing Ireland in the twentieth century because of something which happened in the twelfth?'

'Certainly not. I don't want to govern Ireland a bit. It is much too troublesome. I only wish they would stop moaning about wrongs which never happened. The number of Irishmen massacred by the English is probably exactly equal to the number of Englishmen massacred by the Irish. Why keep sneering about it?'

'Because we have an inferiority complex.'

'Why?'

'Jesus, Mary and Joseph! Have we not been living next door to an Empire for eight hundred years? If your cottage was semi-detached to Buckingham Palace, wouldn't you have an inferiority complex? Wouldn't you have to keep your courage up by repeating that you were quite as good as the Queen?'

'I do see that.'

'And what is biting you, anyway? Are you disliking the Irish because of something which Dev repeats from Mister Sullivan?'

'I do not dislike the Irish.'

'Has anybody here disliked you?'

'Everybody has been absolutely charming to me.'

'Then what's it all about? Don't you realize that all these politicians are ignorant bigots? I might as well denounce the English because I disapprove of Aneurin Bevan.'

('Who isn't an Englishman,' I said promptly.)

'The point is, that whatever the political tub-thumpers may say — whatever bad blood it may suit them to stir up — the ordinary people in the West are what I told you. Simple and innocent. Perhaps it is because they are innocent that the politicians manage to get them excited with that kind of cod.'

'Do you know, Seán, if I did write a book about the West, there would be an odd thing about it.'

'What is that?'

'No comics.'

He thought this over.

'In the East, I daresay there are comical Irishmen, for all I know. They rather exploit their reputation for 'Irish bulls' and funny anecdotes. In the South too. Look at those wonderfully funny stories which my friend Frank O'Connor can write. You know the kind of thing — the horses bolting with the hearse and the coffin full of porter and the corpse abandoned at the left-luggage-office. I never come across anything like that in Mayo.'

'It's a literary tradition which started in the early nineteenth century. The upper classes were writing the novels and the Paddies were the comic relief.'

A bar in Belmullet

'But you are melancholy people really. Have you read Joyce's *Ulysses*?'

'I have so.'

'Except for that one passage when the hierarchy of heaven comes down to the Dublin pub, I think it's the most humourless book I ever read. There is wit and farce and burlesque and satire and irony and all the other kinds of bitter fun, and infinite learning and insight, but not one drop of kindness. Humour has to be kind. Joyce's heart was as cold as a dead fish.'

'There is little compassion in him, perhaps.'

'An austere compassion?'

'It is a tremendous book, for all you say.'

'Yes, and it is true to Ireland. I don't believe that the real Irish do spend all their time filling coffins with porter. They spend a large part of it in sadness and brooding and desperation.'

'We have a hard life in the West.'

'Do you think people will be angry if I say this?'

'No. I think they would be pleased to be treated as grown-ups, instead of babies.'

'As a matter of fact, I agree with what you say about simplicity and innocence and being spontaneous. Will you let me mention another side of the Irish character, which may hurt your feelings?'

'You will mention it in any case.'

'Seán, I suppose you know that ninety per cent of the assassins in America are either Irishmen or Italians? And all the cops are. What on earth is this affinity for violence?'

'It probably has something to do with the desperation you were talking about.'

'Children and savages do smash things.'

'You were not going to treat us as children.'

'Is it some sort of anxiety-neurosis, like what makes people get drunk?'

'It is absolutely true,' said Seán after a bit, 'that the Irish do set less store on the value of human life than the English do. It may be because their lives are actually harder — less valuable. Also, being Catholics, they don't believe that death means extinction. Or perhaps it is just a characteristic of the race.'

'One reason may be that the Romans never penetrated to Ireland. The vast, logical, competent structure of Latin law and civilization was never imposed here. The Gall got it, but the Gael did not. You never had that early training in the habit of discipline and respect for other people's lives.'

'Very well. We are sad, simple, subtle, spontaneous savages, who kill people. What else?'

'You are making it sound horrible.'

'You do not make it sound very complimentary yourself.'

'Are you trying to have a row about it?'

'If you like.'

'Of course I don't like. I would prefer to stay alive.'

'Then what about mentioning something complimentary for a change?'

'I can do that with a will. In the first place, this spontaneity of yours — the continuous, fresh reaction to facts — it makes you more sensitive than the Saxon is. Our laws and discipline make us phlegmatic. We are far too blunt, compared with you. The penetration and finesse of an Irish peasant are ten times sharper than the Englishman's. You are better educated than we are.

'In a way,' I added slowly, 'perhaps you are more civilized.'

'There's a paradox,' said Seán, looking pleased, 'for describing the savages, isn't it?'

'You certainly have an older civilization.'

'Ah, Tim, maybe we'll civilize yourself in the end. I will say you seem to be learning.'

'You are better educated in feelings. Or is it that you have a wider range of feelings? So touchy. But that means you are sensitive to the touch. It's a good thing to be sensitive, isn't it?'

'I would think so.'

'The Irish are more scholarly than the English, more grown-up, more blasé, less credulous. How very strange! I am saying that savages are more adult than civilized people!'

'Civilized people have to have rules, like children at school. We have left the school for children, Tim.'

'Much good has it done you.'

'You are angry yourself, now.'

'No. I must not be. You have been patient with my criticisms, so I must be with yours.'

'It is because,' said Seán teasing, 'my race was civilized by the High Kings of Eriu, while yours was hopping about in woad.'

'I will overlook that.'

'Our bards ...'

'Oh, bother your bards — and also "the island of saints and scholars". You bleat too much about them. It is bad history too. Shall I tell you the most overpowering and unexpected impression which an Englishman gets when he first lands in Dublin?'

'The thumb in the soup plate?'

'Not at all. You know how we always expect you to be dancing a jig with a pig and bashing each other over the head with shillealaghs?'

'Yes.'

'The surprising thing is the silence.'

He looked interested.

'Go to Dublin, and look in the shops and the hotels and the fashionable streets. You will hear loud, exhibitionist cries, hailing and howling at each other in strident voices. All of them are English or American. The quiet talkers, the modest speakers who keep their conversation to themselves, the silent and critical watchers in the corner of the room — these are the native Irish. When an English debutante stops screaming in Jammet's, there is an absolute hush.'

'Perhaps it is the caution of bitter experience,' he said.

'Experience of what?'

'History? Old age? Don't forget, Tim, that we are an ancient race. An Englishman is a recent novelty, compared with the Gael — even if he has outstripped him. When the Americans have finally taken over the British Empire, the English will probably begin to feel a bit elderly too, like us.'

'Are you telling me that you are more grown-up than we are?'

'What do you think?'

I pondered the strange relationships of humanity, gazing into the turf fire. It had stopped smoking. It glowed softly, like an incandescent rose petal, its lovely scent tickling the inside, upper tips of our noses. The amber, Irish whisky in our glasses was tart and bracing — not sugary like the adulterated Scotch.

'There is another thing I want to get off my chest. You know those hateful books about the Troubles, like the one ...'

'Leave out its name,' he said. 'Don't think about it. Don't

write about these things. Besides, what did the Black and Tans and the I.R.A. do to each other, compared with the fascists and communists and the Jewish massacres we have now? Leave it to the swine to dig up the swinishness. Don't start arguments which can only be bitter. Civilized people have to forget and try to be decent.

'After all,' he added kindly, 'your people did not do so badly as a master race — not compared with Stalin and Hitler. I'll admit that. Yes, I'll admit that.'